P9-DGL-145

HENRY LOUIS GATES, JR.

Recent Titles in Greenwood Biographies

Oprah Winfrey: A Biography
Helen S. Garson

John F. Kennedy: A Biography
Michael Meagher and Larry D. Gragg

Maya Lin: A Biography
Donald Langmead

Stonewall Jackson: A Biography
Ethan S. Rafuse

Rosa Parks: A Biography
Joyce A. Hanson

Emiliano Zapata: A Biography
Albert Rolls

Diego Rivera: A Biography
Manuel Aguilar-Moreno and Erika Cabrera

Ronald Reagan: A Biography
J. David Woodard

Pancho Villa: A Biography
Alejandro Quintana

Michelle Obama: A Biography
Alma Halbert Bond

Lady Gaga: A Biography
Paula Johanson

Bono: A Biography
David Kootnikoff

HENRY LOUIS GATES, JR.

A Biography

Meg Greene

GREENWOOD BIOGRAPHIES

AN IMPRINT OF ABC-CLIO, LLC
Santa Barbara, California • Denver, Colorado • Oxford, England

Library of Congress Cataloging-in-Publication Data

Greene, Meg.
Henry Louis Gates, Jr. : a biography / Meg Greene.
pages cm. — (Greenwood biographies)
Includes bibliographical references and index.
ISBN 978–0–313–38046–4 (hardback) — ISBN 978–0–313–38047–1 (ebook)
1. Gates, Henry Louis. 2. African American scholars—Biography. 3. Critics—United States—Biography. I. Title.
PS29.G28G74 2012
810.9′896073—dc23
[B] 2012000201

ISBN: 978–0–313–38046–4
EISBN: 978–0–313–38047–1

16 15 14 13 12 1 2 3 4 5

This book is also available on the World Wide Web as an eBook.
Visit www.abc-clio.com for details.

Greenwood
An Imprint of ABC-CLIO, LLC

ABC-CLIO, LLC
130 Cremona Drive, P.O. Box 1911
Santa Barbara, California 93116-1911

This book is printed on acid-free paper ∞

Manufactured in the United States of America

CONTENTS

SERIES FOREWORD

In response to school and library needs, ABC-CLIO publishes this distinguished series of full-length biographies specifically for student use. Prepared by field experts and professionals, these engaging biographies are tailored for students who need challenging yet accessible biographies. Ideal for school assignments and student research, the length, format, and subject areas are designed to meet educators' requirements and students' interests.

ABC-CLIO offers an extensive selection of biographies spanning all curriculum-related subject areas, including social studies, the sciences, literature and the arts, history and politics, and popular culture, covering public figures and famous personalities from all time periods and backgrounds, both historic and contemporary, who have made an impact on American and/or world culture. The subjects of these biographies were chosen based on comprehensive feedback from librarians and educators. Consideration was given to both curriculum relevance and inherent interest. Readers will find a wide array of subject choices from fascinating entertainers like Miley Cyrus and Lady Gaga to inspiring leaders like John F. Kennedy and Nelson Mandela, from the greatest athletes of our time like Michael Jordan and Lance Armstrong to the most amazing success stories of our day like J.K. Rowling and Oprah.

While the emphasis is on fact, not glorification, the books are meant to be fun to read. Each volume provides in-depth information about the subject's life from birth through childhood, the teen years, and adulthood. A thorough account relates family background and education, traces personal and professional influences, and explores struggles, accomplishments, and contributions. A timeline highlights the most significant life events against a historical perspective. Bibliographies supplement the reference value of each volume.

INTRODUCTION

> I liken the role of the scholar of African American studies today to a Talmudic scholar, someone whose job it is to preserve the tradition, to resurrect the texts and key events of the past and to explicate them. I've always thought of myself as both a literary historian and a literary critic, someone who loves archives and someone who is dedicated to resurrecting texts that have dropped out of sight. As it turns out, there are a huge number of those texts. At the beginning of my career I didn't realize quite how many there were.
>
> —Henry Louis Gates, 2002 National Endowment for the Humanities interview

For Henry Louis Gates, Jr., the quest for knowledge, no matter the outcome, has been the basis of his long career. His keen appreciation for the written word, coupled with his own vitality and openness in his approach to literature, has made Gates one of the premier literary critics and scholars of the late 20th and early 21st centuries. His centrist approach, which embraces Western thought while at the same time championing the diverse, the vernacular, and even to some the profane, has also made him one of the more provocative academic thinkers of his time. As one profile noted, this approach is what makes Gates and his work so important, in that he overlooks nothing that will promise a vibrant and lively engaging discussion of culture. Absolutism, in the world of Henry Louis Gates, Jr. has no place.

Flashy, entrepreneurial, self-promoting, and outspoken, Gates sometimes comes across more celebrity figure than academic, for which his colleagues in academia frequently criticize him. He is wealthy, powerful, and elitist and has been seen by some black activists as having abandoned efforts to help the less fortunate. Tomas Jaehn of Stanford University observes about Gates's position: "Some of the critics fail to understand the little-analyzed role of a public intellectual in an academic environment (or an academic intellectual in the public limelight[1]) . . ." His work has widened the acceptance of African American studies and has given it more recognition and respectability as a serious field of study. It should not come as a surprise that along with Gates's visibility, national interest in African American studies has increased noticeably.

In his essay "The Talented Tenth," W.E.B. Du Bois, noted African American writer and thinker, wrote, "The Negro Race, like all races, is going to be saved by its exceptional men. The problem of education then, among Negroes, must first of all deal with the 'Talented Tenth.' It is the problem of developing the best of this race that they may guide the Mass away from the contamination and death of the worst." For Henry Louis Gates, this quest to be among the best has been a constant theme throughout his life. His curiosity about the greater world has led him on a journey that not only taught him about that world but has also allowed Gates to open the door for thousands of others to people, places, and ideas that have contributed mightily to expanding our knowledge of the history and contributions of African Americans to our own history. Gates's own quest to learn about the nations of Africa as a young boy led him to journeys through that continent many times; some of those trips have been made with a camera crew in tow in order to share his discoveries with others. Lastly, Gates's search to learn more about his family and its origins has made it possible for many African Americans to learn more about their roots as well.

At one point in his life, Gates entertained thoughts of becoming a doctor. Although there is little doubt that Gates would have been a fine physician, his decision to pursue the study of literature and history has been most profound. His work and his continuing efforts to make American literature and history a more complete entity have opened up the way for other students and scholars to pursue avenues that at one time would have remained hidden from the American literary canon. And in doing so, Henry Louis Gates offers, and challenges us to pursue the quest for knowledge with as much enthusiasm and excitement as he has for all of his life.

NOTE

1. Henry Louis Gates, Jr., Stanford Presidential Lectures in the Humanities and Arts, http://prelectur.stanford.edu/lecturers/gates/.

TIMELINE: EVENTS IN THE LIFE OF HENRY LOUIS GATES, JR.

1950	Born Louis Smith Gates in Keyser, West Virginia.
1968	Graduates from high school, enrolls at Potomac State College.
1969	Enters Yale University.
1970	Travels to Tanzania to work in mission hospital.
1973	Graduates summa cum laude from Yale with a degree in history; begins studies at Clare College, Cambridge University, England; begins work as a correspondent for *Time* magazine.
1974	Graduates with an MA in English language and literature from Cambridge.
1975	Returns to the United States, works in the Afro-American studies department at Yale.
1976–1979	Becomes Lecturer in English and Afro-American Studies at Yale.
1979	Receives PhD in English language and literature from Cambridge; marries Sharon Lynn Adams and changes name legally to Henry Louis Gates, Jr.

1979–1984	Appointed Assistant Professor of English and Afro-American Studies, Yale University.
1980	Begins work on Black Periodical Literature Project.
1981	Receives MacArthur "Genius" Grant.
1983	Discovers *Our Nig.*
1984–1985	Appointed Associate Assistant Professor of English and Afro-American Studies at Yale; *Black Literature and Literary Theory* is published.
1985	Is denied tenure at Yale; takes job as Professor of English, Comparative Literature and Africana Studies at Cornell University, undertakes publishing of the magazine *Transition.*
1988	Named W.E.B. Du Bois Professor of Literature at Cornell; *Schomburg Library of Nineteenth-Century Black Women Writers* is published.
1989	*Signifying Monkey* is published; wins American Book Award and Anisfield-Wolf Book Award for Race Relations.
1990	Appointed John Spencer Bassett Professor of English and Literature, Duke University; defends 2 Live Crew at obscenity trial in Florida; *Norton Anthology of African American Literature* is published.
1991	Accepts job at Harvard as W.E.B. Du Bois Professor of Humanities and Director, W.E.B. Du Bois Institute for Afro-American Research, and Chairman of the Afro-American Studies Department.
1992	Elected to the American Academy of Arts and Sciences.
1994	Publishes *Colored People: A Memoir.*
1997	Named by *Time* magazine as one of the "25 Most Influential Americans."
1998	Films *Wonders of the African World*; receives National Medal of Arts and the National Humanities Medal.
1999	*Africana: The Encyclopedia of the African and African American Experience* is published, work will be released on CD as the *Encarta Africana.*

2000	Wins NAACP Image Award, Outstanding Literary Work, Nonfiction, for book, *Wonders of the African World.*
2001	*Bondswoman's Narrative* is discovered by Gates.
2002	Selected by the National Endowment for the Humanities as its Jefferson Lecturer.
2006	Hosts PBS series *African American Lives*; inducted into the Sons of the American Revolution.
2008	Founds *The Root*, an online magazine.
2009	Arrested at home by Cambridge policeman; receives the Ralph Lowell Award from the Corporation for Public Broadcasting, the highest honor in the field of public television; hosts PBS series *Looking for Lincoln.*
2010	Hosts series *Faces of America.*

Chapter 1

"SEPIA TIME"

Situated in the upper northeast tip of West Virginia, along the North Branch Potomac River and near the Maryland border, is the tiny town of Piedmont. Chartered in 1856 in Mineral County, the town was the creation of the New Creek Company. The company's primary business was that of transportation, and the New Creek Company was instrumental in the building of canals and railroads. The company also purchased land and set up manufacturing facilities. The town derived its name from the location near the foothills of the Allegheny Mountains. Convinced of Piedmont's potential as a transportation center, the town fathers persuaded the Baltimore and Ohio Railroad, as well as a number of other railway companies, to use coal, of which there was a plentiful supply around the town, instead of wood to run their locomotives.

Almost from the beginning, Piedmont's economy was tied to the Baltimore & Ohio (B&O) Railroad. With the expansion of coal and iron mining in the Cumberland basin, branch line railroads were needed. The town's location proved an excellent site for the eastern terminus for the B&O rail line. However, by the end of the 1870s, with the rapid growth of rail traffic west of the Ohio River and with the increased need for coal from the northern mining area of West Virginia, the Baltimore and Ohio Railroad needed more room to build additional shipping and repair facilities. Because Piedmont could not meet the needs of the railroad, new facilities were built farther down at New Creek Station, now the town of Keyser, West Virginia. Piedmont's fortunes continued to worsen when, in 1916, the railroad demolished the existing shop complex.

Although the focus of the town was the railroad, some of Piedmont's more enterprising citizenry saw other possibilities. Henry G. Davis, a station agent of the B&O at Piedmont, took a gamble and opened the first store in Piedmont. Relying on an extensive bartering system, Davis also began acquiring undeveloped coal and timberlands in exchange for goods from his store. In 1858, Davis resigned his position at the B&O to establish H. G. Davis & Company, which among other enterprises included the Piedmont Savings Bank. Thirty years later, in 1888, William Luke established the West Virginia Paper Company (now the NewPage Corporation) in the area known as West Piedmont. The paper company would go on to become one of the area's largest employers for both its white and black residents. The company dominated not only the town's economy but its air as well; on particularly hot and humid days, the air reeked of a rotten egg smell that wafted from the plant. Those who objected to the odor were reminded that it "smells like money,"[1] a potent illustration of how important the paper company was to the local economy.

LIFE IN PIEDMONT

Between the late 1850s and the late 1880s, Piedmont offered the promise of employment first with the railroad and then with the paper company. As a result, immigrants from Ireland and Italy found their way to the tiny community. Similarly, African Americans in search of better jobs and a better life also settled in Piedmont. Still, longstanding racial attitudes prevailed. Although the immigrants performed a variety of tasks at the paper mill, almost every African American who worked there was consigned outside at the loading docks.

Despite its small population, Piedmont maintained a strict, almost unspoken social and racial hierarchy. At the top were the wealthy whites who lived in the fine Victorian frame and brick houses on Hampshire Street, surrounded by the white and black middle-class and working-class neighborhoods. African Americans congregated in one of three locales: "Downtown" located on Back Street, which was also known as "Black Street"; Erin Street, also known as "Up on the Hill"; and Rat Tail Road.

Beneath the surface of small-town life, there existed racism and segregation, not written into codes or laws, but, as both the blacks and whites understood, a world woven into the "condition of existence" that offered both a sense of security and belonging as well as of isolation and intimidation. During the 1950s, Piedmont was no hotbed of racial unrest. Yet, like much of the rest of the country, the daily contact between blacks and whites was a carefully choreographed dance that determined where one could go and where one could not. Blacks in Piedmont did not own their own homes, lived in one of the clearly demarcated black neighborhoods, and ate standing up at the Cut-Rate, the town's local restaurant.[2]

As in the rest of the United States, the racial climate in Piedmont during the 1950s reflected both the hard-fought progress against racial discrimination and the necessary accommodations made with it in the interest of survival. At first oppressed by slavery and later, after the Civil War, by the "Jim Crow" laws, which legalized discrimination based on race, African Americans found themselves the inhabitants of a nation that would not protect their rights. The legal barriers to freedom and equal opportunity that blacks faced were often reinforced with extralegal intimidation and violence.

By the early decades of the twentieth century, organized efforts by African Americans to overturn Jim Crow laws led to the formation of a number of organizations that mounted legal challenges to racial segregation and racial discrimination. Perhaps the most important of these was the National Association for the Advancement of Colored People (NAACP), created in 1909. Yet it would not be until the end of World War II in 1945 that organizations such as the NAACP began to see the success of their long campaign to overturn racist legislation. By 1950, the civil rights movement was poised to challenge discrimination not only in the courts but also in the streets with the promise that blacks would attain equality in all areas of American life, including employment, education, and housing. The movement also sought to protect African Americans' right to vote and to strike down once and for all segregated facilities that included schools, restaurants, hospitals, railroad cars, buses, and the like, which had been in place since 1896 when, in the case of *Plessy v. Ferguson*, the Supreme Court of the United States had rules that separate public facilities for blacks were, indeed, equal. Their efforts marked the beginnings of a turbulent decade in American life.[3]

In Piedmont, West Virginia, the civil rights movement would seem as foreign as an overseas conflict. As Henry Louis Gates, Jr., reflected, whites and African Americans got along fairly well in Piedmont, as long as African Americans stayed in their customary place and occupied their customary roles, not shopping at the white grocery store, not sitting down and eating pizza at the local restaurant, not moving into white neighborhoods, and not trying to secure loans at the local bank. "Other than that," wrote Gates, "colored and white got along pretty well."[4]

ORIGINS AND ANTECEDENTS

In 1950, the Supreme Court abolished segregated railroad cars. Orlando, Florida, hired its first African American police officers. Chuck Cooper, Nathaniel Clifton, and Earl Lloyd became the first African American basketball players for the National Basketball Association (NBA). And African American political scientist and diplomat Dr. Ralph Bunche received the Nobel Peace Prize. It was also the year that Louis Smith Gates was born on September 16, in Keyser, West Virginia, a small city situated to the east of Piedmont, where his parents and relatives lived. Louis was the second child and second son for Henry and Pauline Gates; their eldest son, Paul Edward, nicknamed "Rocky," had been born in 1945. Gates's birth name caused him some consternation. Pauline had originally promised to name her second child at the request of a girlfriend. Growing up, Gates hated the name "Smith," believing that it deprived him of his birthright. He eventually told his parents how he felt, and before his marriage in 1979, had his name legally changed to Henry Louis Gates, Jr.

Gates grew up in the midst of a family that had a strong sense of its roots. As an adult, he learned that his family tree extended as far back as 1753. "I learned about my ancestor John Redman, a Free Negro who fought in the Revolutionary War," Gates explained in a 2009 interview. "He mustered into the Continental Army on Christmas Day in 1778 and mustered out in 1784." Redman married a free black woman, and the couple eventually settled in Moorefield, West Virginia, where they owned property. Another interesting aspect of Gates family history is that he is descended from seven sets of ancestors who were all free by 1823 in West Virginia.[5]

The noticeable absence of slavery in the Eastern Panhandle of West Virginia was due to the fact that there weren't large farms or plantations such as those in Virginia or North and South Carolina. In addition, those free men and women of color often owned property. Gates's father, Henry Louis Gates, Sr., was descended from slaves who were owned by a Maryland planter by the name of Horatio Gates, whose land holdings included property in what is now Berkeley Springs, West Virginia. His father was nicknamed "Heinie" because he was so light-skinned he could pass for white. Henry Sr.'s grandfather, Edward Gates, was the eldest son of a black slave mother, Jane Gates, a laundress, and white planter named Brady. Based on census records, sometime between 1860 and 1870, Jane Gates received a large parcel of land from Brady that became the 200-acre family farm known as Gates Point near Patterson Creek in Mineral County, West Virginia. According to family descriptions, the farm was a beautiful acreage filled with hills and fields, in which deer, rabbits, turkeys, and squirrels were plentiful. Patterson Creek, an offshoot of the South Branch of the Potomac River, meandered through the farmland, its waters bursting with trout and bass. It was an idyllic homestead for the Gates family.[6]

Edward Gates went on to marry a woman by the name of Maude Fortune. Together they had four children, one of whom was Henry Sr.'s father, "Pop" Gates. The Gates family continued to live on the farm until the 1920s, when the property was sold and the family moved to Cumberland, Maryland. Pop Gates and his father went into business together, establishing a cleaning service that cleaned offices of the businesses on Main Street in Cumberland and a chimney-stoking service that sent workers out to light furnaces and haul away ashes. Maude was no less diligent; in 1890, she founded St. Phillip's Episcopal Church and helped recruit priests from Haiti and Jamaica. She was also the first black in Cumberland to subscribe to W.E.B. Du Bois's magazine, *Crisis*. She was also, by 1919, Cumberland's only socialist.

By all accounts, Maude Fortune Gates was a formidable woman. Believing strongly in the importance of education, Maude saw to it that her three daughters were properly schooled in Washington. All three girls eventually went on to college and enjoyed successful careers. Their children also followed in their mothers' footsteps. However, Maude's aspirations for her son were much lower; instead of education in a classroom, she forced Pop Gates to work the farm until the property was sold. Pop Gates eventually married Gertrude Helen Redman, with whom he had seven sons. Of those seven, only the youngest, Henry Sr., would attend school for a short time in New Jersey, where he aspired to become a priest; his brothers went to work in factories.

Henry Sr. would marry Pauline Augusta Coleman, one of 12 children born to "Daddy Paul" and "Biggie" Coleman. Daddy Paul worked a variety of jobs, including as a handyman, to support his growing family. Despite his modest occupation, Daddy Paul and his family were well respected, with strong ties to Piedmont; both whites and blacks in the community thought highly of the family. Because of their reputation, the family would enjoy a number of "firsts" in the community: the first blacks allowed to own guns and hunt on white-owned property, the first to become Eagle Scouts, the first black family to own their property, and the first from Piedmont to send their children to college. The family was also extremely devout. Unlike the Gates relatives who enjoyed drinking, playing cards, and solving crossword puzzles, among other frivolous activities, the Colemans were religious, often self-righteous, and rarely mixed with the other black families in Piedmont. Unlike the Gateses, though, who tended to get together only when a family member died, the Colemans were renowned for their annual family reunions, considered to be one of the most important social events of the year. As Gates recalled, one had to be a Coleman to be invited; this designation did not extend to in-laws. Beginning in 1949, and always on the last Sunday in July, the

Coleman relatives would gather on an acre of farmland near Patterson's Creek or at the South Branch of the Potomac River to eat, play games such as badminton and softball, swim in the nearby river, and talk. The end of the day's festivities was always signaled by the careful cutting of a watermelon by one of the uncles. After that, everything was packed up, the grounds cleaned, and, one by one, the families slipped away back to Piedmont. Despite Gates's reservations about his mother's side of the family, he still counted the annual family get-togethers and holidays at his grandmother Coleman's among his earliest and happiest childhood memories.[7]

CHILDHOOD

Henry Louis Gates, Jr. remembers his early childhood with a great degree of fondness. As he later recalled in a 2009 interview, "Piedmont was the center of the world for me. It was fantastic. I loved growing up in West Virginia."[8] The Gates family lived in a tiny three-room house on Fredlock Street, not far from Pauline's mother. Not long after Henry Jr. was born, Rocky was sent to live with his grandmother, a common practice during that time, given the limitations of space and the time devoted to a newborn baby. Like his brother, Henry also had a nickname: "Skippy." In an interview in 1994, Gates explained the origin of the name, stating that, "From the time I was born—the day I was born, my Uncle Raymond called me Skipper, and then it became Skippy. We were Piedmonts on the river—Piedmont, West Virginia, is on the Potomac River, two hours west of Washington, so there's a whole Marine mentality there, and so I became 'The Skipper.' " However, in another interview, Gates stated that it was his mother who had given him the nickname, often calling him "Skippy Boy" or "Skipper Ripper Dipper."[9]

By the time Gates turned four, the family moved over to Pearl Street near Rat Tail Road, where his father had rented a larger house for his family. The daily routine varied little in their new home. Every day except Sunday, Henry Sr. left for his job at the paper mill at 6:30 AM. He worked until 3:30 PM. Family dinner was on the table by 4 PM, after which Henry Sr. left for his second job as a janitor at the offices of the telephone company. By 7:30, Gates's father would return home, where the family would watch television together. Henry Sr. was also an avid reader, especially of crime and mystery stories, as well as an avid baseball and sports fan.

Pauline Gates contributed to the family income by cleaning houses when she was not at home taking care of her family. Early on, Pauline developed a special bond with her youngest child. Some of Gates's earliest memories of his mother are of the time they spent in the kitchen, where she cooked and sewed. Gates spent hours playing with the Betsy McCall paper dolls that were found in the women's magazine, or with puppets or marionettes. Among the boy's two favorite toys were a Jerry Mahoney ventriloquist dummy, based on a popular television character, and a dancing black minstrel puppet called Dancing Dan. It was also in the kitchen that Gates first learned to read and write with his mother's help.

In order to expose her children more to the world outside of Piedmont, Pauline subscribed to *Jack & Jill*, a popular magazine for young children, so her sons could see how children "outside the Valley" looked and lived. Gates's father would also look at the magazine, especially at the black children that were portrayed, and commented, "They handpicked those children. No dummies, no nappy hair, heads not too kinky, lips not too thick, no disses and no dats."[10]

At the age of four, Gates gave his first public performance, a memory that has stayed with him all his adult life:

> It was a religious program, at which each of the children of the Sunday school was to deliver a "piece"—as the people in our church referred to a religious recitation. Mine was the couplet "Jesus was a boy like me,/And like Him I want to be. . . ." So, after weeks of practice in elocution, hair pressed and greased down, shirt starched and pants pressed, I was ready to give my piece. I remember skipping along to the church with all of the other kids, driving everyone crazy, repeating that couplet over and over. . . . Finally we made it to the church, and it was packed. . . . Because I was the youngest child on the program, I was the first to go. And then the worst happened: I completely forgot the words of my piece. Standing there, pressed and starched, just as clean as I could be, in front of just about everybody in our part of town,

> I could not for the life of me remember one word of that piece. After standing there I don't know how long, struck dumb and captivated by all of those staring eyes, I heard a voice from near the back of the church proclaim, "Jesus was a boy like me,/And like Him I want to be." And my mother, having arisen to find my voice, smoothed her dress and sat down again. The congregation's applause lasted as long as its laughter as I crawled back to my seat.

For Henry, this moment captured for him what he would attempt to do with his own work in the years to come: "much of my scholarly and critical work has been an attempt to learn how to speak in the strong, compelling cadences of my mother's voice."[11]

Gates also credits his mother with building self-confidence in both him and his older brother. In a 2003 interview, he stated, "She reinforced it over and over and over again that, in her opinion, we were beautiful and brilliant and whatever else. And I don't know if any of those things were true, but if someone says it to you every day like a mantra, you become hypnotized by that. . . . My mother bred a tremendous amount of intellectual self-confidence in my brother and me, and we always knew that we would be loved no matter what."[12]

From a young age, Gates showed an intense interest in food. For instance, Sundays meant attending church and then returning home for Sunday dinner. While Gates and his brother were in Sunday school, Pauline was at home busily preparing the family's Sunday dinner. The menu varied little from week to week: fried chicken, mashed potatoes, green beans, corn pudding, gravy, rolls, a lettuce salad with sliced tomatoes and egg. When Gates traveled with his father and brother to baseball games in Pittsburgh, it was as much for the draw of the stadium food such as the hot dogs, popcorn, and candy, as it was for the journey, the game, and the time spent with his father and brother. One of his favorite activities was getting up early to have breakfast with his father. While eating, he often reached over to grab a piece of egg or potato from his father's plate, believing that somehow his father's food always tasted better than his own. He would even drink coffee like his father, though his father would tell him that "Coffee will make you black," a reference to Gates's light complexion.[13]

Gates's love of food and aversion to playing sports, while gratifying to his mother, made him fat. It also led to his being called a number of unfortunate nicknames. While his mother viewed his stature as husky, his father and brother called him names such as Two-ton Tony Galento or Chicken Flinsterwall. By the time he entered school, his size led his classmates to call him Hoss Cartwright, a reference to a heavyset popular character on the popular television show *Bonanza*. Adding further insult to injury, Gates was cursed with flat arches, which meant he had to wear special corrective shoes. Even though his mother thought the blunt-ended, round-toed Stride-Rite shoes with special soles were "elegant," Henry Jr. despised them and called them instead "Stride-wrongs."[14]

Despite the problems with his weight and his feet, Gates had, for the most part, a happy childhood. As he later wrote in his memoir, *Colored People*:

> I was short and round. . . . Still, I was clean and energetic, and most of the time I was cheerful. And I liked to play with other kids, not so much because I enjoyed the things we did together but because I could watch them be happy.[15]

GROWING AWARENESS

For most of his childhood, Henry Louis Gates, Jr. could not eat in most public restaurants, stay an overnight in most hotels, use bathrooms that were not marked "colored," or walk into a white department store to try on clothes. Libraries, parks, and all public transportation were also all segregated, either keeping blacks out entirely or confining them to "colored only" sections. Even the company picnics at the paper plant were segregated. Particularly galling to him was going to the local restaurant, the Cut-Rate, where he had to watch blacks standing up to eat their food on paper plates and drink in plastic glasses, while whites ate off china dishes and drank from glasses while sitting comfortably in the restaurant booths. Ironically, the house rules at the Cut-Rate were bent for one person: Henry Louis Sr., who his son believed was allowed to sit down and eat in the restaurant in part because of his light complexion and because he was often there to pick up orders for employees of the phone company, customers the restaurant's owner dearly needed. During the first years of his life, however, white people were a shadowy presence for Gates. The only whites he encountered were either authority figures such as the mill bosses or those few who occasionally braved the color line to visit the black V.F.W. or who showed up at a party or dance. On those occasions, Gates recounts, the feeling he had was that somehow the "borders" of the black world had been breached and even violated. It was for him an unpleasant situation.

In trying to understand the larger segregated world in which he lived, Gates also began noticing differences in his own smaller, more comfortable community. Skin color, for instance, was an ongoing topic of discussion among his community. One legacy of slavery was that those who were mulattos, octoroons, or quadroons, whose ancestors had been fathered by whites and born of slave mothers, enjoyed greater advantages in everything from position to living arrangements. For many blacks, having a light complexion became a very important sign of status and privilege to the point that some would bleach their skin. At a Coleman Thanksgiving dinner, when looking at his relatives, Gates began to understand the meaning of the phrase "colored" people: "their colors ran the full spectrum of brown, like the whole race in miniature, from the richest darkest chocolate to the creamiest café au lait." Whereas the Coleman side of the family tended to be darker skinned, Gates also noticed that on his father's side of the family, the complexions tended to be lighter, so much so that in some cases, his father's relatives were assumed to be white. In fact, many members of the Gates family qualified as octoroons, that is, people whose ancestry is considered to be one-eighth African, or as Henry Louis Sr., explained "light, bright, and damn near white."[16]

Hair was another topic to receive considerable discussion. "In my community we were obsessed with hair," Gates recounted in an interview.

> Having straight hair became very important to people as a status symbol, and so often they straightened their hair, or if they didn't straighten their hair—[they] would put different kind of pomades on it, different kinds of oils, as we would call it, which basically was very thick grease, and brush it or wear a stocking cap to make

your hair appear more naturally wavy, as we would put it, than it really was.

It seems that everyone Gates knew wanted "good" hair, that is, hair that was shiny and wavy as opposed to "bad" hair that was kinky.[17]

"COLORED, COLORED ON CHANNEL TWO"

Compared to the rest of the country, Piedmont seemed behind the times in many ways. One way to keep up with what was going on in society at large was by watching television. Not only did watching television offer the opportunity for the Gates family to be together, it also opened up a window into another world. As Gates later recalled in an interview, "you would watch television till 9:30 or 10, whenever our bedtime was. And my dad would do a running commentary on whatever we saw on television. . . . And in between reading and looking at the TV, and we'd do our homework."[18]

With the exception of televised sports events, such as baseball games or boxing matches, television during the early 1950s offered little in the way of showcasing African Americans. Instead, the television was filled with images of whites; in fact, Gates later stated that it was through television that he began to get to "know" white people as "people." Evening hours were spent watching such programs as *Superman*, *Lassie*, *I Love Lucy*, *Broken Arrow*, *Father Knows Best*, *Dragnet*, and *Ozzie and Harriet*. The program *The Life of Riley* was a particular favorite in the Gates household because the main character worked in a factory like Henry Louis Sr. Shows that depicted the wealthy, such as *Topper*, offered a tantalizing glimpse of what life might be like in the homes on East Hampshire Street in Piedmont.[19]

Leave It to Beaver, a television series about a young boy, his older brother, and parents was also popular with the young Gates. The world of Mayfield, where the Cleaver family lived, was an ideal that Henry and his family strived to attain but that was always out of reach. The Cleavers' house and neighborhood were the kind of places where the Gates family would have liked to live; the office where Ward Cleaver worked was where Henry Louis Sr. ought to have worked. *Leave It to Beaver* offered a hard lesson in reality the show's creators had not intended to deliver, for watching it make Gates realize that such programs depicted a world in which white people owned their own houses and enjoyed a standard of living that most African American families could not even imagine, much less attain. Yet, with the changes the civil rights movement brought, those very ideals would be far closer to becoming a reality for Gates and his brother, if not for his parents.

By far the most popular program of all in the Gates household was *Amos and Andy*, a situation comedy set in an African American community. The program was the first television series with an all-black cast. Despite many complaints in the black community that the program was based on stereotypes demeaning to blacks, many African Americans looked forward to watching a program that depicted life in a black world, with black businessmen, doctors, lawyers, teachers, undertakers, and judges—occupations that many dreamed of entering or at least living to see their children enter. As Gates stated, the world that Amos and Andy occupied "was *all* colored, just like ours."[20]

Apart from *Amos and Andy*, there were few opportunities to watch African Americans on television. And when they did unexpectedly appear, it was a special event in the black community. The cries of "Colored, colored, on Channel Two," would send one person to the phone or another to the porch to alert the neighborhood where to tune in the appropriate channel. Movies with African American actors meant special permission to stay up late to watch the television. When singer Nat King Cole became the first African American to host his own program, Gates remembers

> all the members of our family gather[ed] around the TV to watch it . . . neighbors came to watch it. I mean, it was a real test for the race. I mean, would we be able to pull this off? It was a major breakthrough. . . . Whenever there was a black person on TV, we rooted for him like you'd root for your home team.[21]

If African Americans were in short supply on the television, they were more accessible on the radio. Many a night, after their parents had gone to bed, the two Gates brothers fell asleep in their bunk beds listening to radio programs on Rocky's tiny transistor radio such as *Randy's Record Shop*, which broadcast from Gallatin, Tennessee.

The program aired the music of such black performers such as the Platters, Howlin' Wolf, or Joe Turner. In a 1994 radio interview, Gates described listening to the radio:

> You couldn't get it [during] the day. You could only get it at night. It was on AM. It was very scratchy, but you would solder your radio dial to its point on the dial and listen to it every night. . . . And it was great. It was an aspect of black culture that I didn't encounter in my daily life. I remember ads for things like Black Strap Laxatives, and they would sing the song just like you would sing blues or rhythm and blues. So it was very important to me. Then you could—as you know, then you could order the records. So we would order these 45s through "Randy's Record Shop" which, again, we could not get in our local record stores. My first encounter with black music on a national scale. . . . You certainly weren't getting it through WKYR or whatever it was called in Keyser, West Virginia. I mean, basically, I was raised with country music, hillbilly music.[22]

A CHANGING WORLD

Nothing could have been as vastly different from the idyllic world of *Leave It to Beaver* and *The Ozzie and Harriet Show* as watching current events on the television. By 1955, the country was undergoing great social and political changes, particularly as the civil rights movement gained momentum in the South. In the world of television, the drama and vivid images unfolding in cities and towns across the South were too compelling to ignore. Little wonder that newscasts were now expanding to include live telecasts of these important events. Gates and his family watched the news every night to see what was happening. For Gates, the stories unfolding on the screen were as momentous as "watching the Olympics or the World Series when somebody colored was on." Among his first memories were watching the coverage of the murder of 15-year-old Emmett Till in Mississippi and the subsequent trial of two white men for the crime. In 1957, all eyes in the black community of Piedmont were glued to the television watching five black students in Little Rock, Arkansas, being escorted to the

Little Rock High School by National Guardsman, symbolizing the end of a segregated education in the United States. "Civil Rights took us by surprise," Gates recalled many years after those events. Still, for those blacks in Piedmont, the dawn of the civil rights era could be no more than a spectator sport until the verdict in *Brown v. Board of Education* in 1954. On May 17, 1954, the United States Supreme Court stated that the segregation of white and black children in public schools had a detrimental effect upon black children. Separate schools, the court ruled, were not equal, and thus the practice of segregated education, legally in place since 1896, was unconstitutional. As a consequence of this decision, the Court ordered that segregation be phased out over time, "with all deliberate speed." As it did for all African Americans, the *Brown* decision would have enormous implications for everyone in the Gates family.[23]

NOTES

1. Henry Louis Gates, *Colored People* (New York: Vintage Books, 1995), 6.
2. Ibid., 8.
3. "Civil Rights Movement." *Gale Encyclopedia of U.S. Economic History*. Gale Group, 1999. Reproduced in History Resource Center. Farmington Hills, MI: Gale. http://galenet.galegroup.com/servlet/HistRC/.
4. Gates, *Colored People*, 28.
5. "West Virginia Celebrates Its Historymakers," http://www.wvcommerce.org/people/successstories/wvhistorymakers/default.aspx.
6. Gates, *Colored People*, 71–74; Henry Louis Gates, Jr., "Who's Your (Irish) Daddy?" *The Root*, http://www.theroot.com/views/whos-your-irish-daddy.
7. Gates, *Colored People*, 65.
8. "West Virginia Celebrates Its Historymakers," http://www.wvcommerce.org/people/successstories/wvhistorymakers/default.aspx.
9. "Booknotes: Colored People by Henry Louis Gates, Jr.," October 9, 1994, http://www.booknotes.org/Watch/60633-1/Henry+Louis+Gates.aspx; Cheryl Bentsen, "Head Negro in Charge," *Boston Magazine*, July 23, 2009, http://www.bostonmagazine.com/articles/Henry_Louis_Gates_Jr/page1.

10. Cheryl Bentsen, "Head Negro in Charge," *Boston Magazine*, July 23, 2009, http://www.bostonmagazine.com/articles/Henry_Louis_Gates_Jr/page1.

11. Henry Louis Gates, "Whose Canon Is It Anyway?" *The New York Times*, February 26, 1989, Section 7, 1.

12. Voices against Indifference Initiative: "Henry Louis Gates, Jr.: W.E.B. Du Bois and the Encyclopedia Africana." http://www.echofoundation.org/Past%20Projects%20II/Gates/Biography.htm.

13. Gates, *Colored People*, 79–81.

14. Ibid., 80.

15. Ibid., 80.

16. Ibid., 73.

17. "Booknotes: Colored People by Henry Louis Gates, Jr.," October 9, 1994, http://www.booknotes.org/Watch/60633-1/Henry+Louis+Gates.aspx.

18. Ibid.

19. Gates, *Colored People*, 20.

20. Ibid., 20.

21. "Booknotes: Colored People by Henry Louis Gates, Jr.," October 9, 1994, http://www.booknotes.org/Watch/60633-1/Henry+Louis+Gates.aspx.

22. Ibid.

23. Gates, *Colored People*, 25; Landmark Cases of the Supreme Court: *Brown v. Board of Education*, http://www.streetlaw.org/en/Case.6.aspx.

Chapter 2
SCHOOL DAYS

Even with a long history of protest, it was not until the 1950s that African Americans began making serious progress in their struggle for equal rights. With the historic 1954 Supreme Court decision in *Brown v. Board of Education* that outlawed the 1896 *Plessy v. Ferguson* doctrine of "separate but equal," African Americans realized that the time was right to end the specter of Jim Crow and discrimination. One of the best ways to move forward was to improve the quality of education for black children, allowing them the opportunity to better themselves. The importance of the *Brown* decision cannot be underestimated; at last, the foundations of segregation were beginning to crumble. The court had set in motion the gradual dismantling of legal segregation against African Americans.

In the Gates household in Piedmont, West Virginia, it was as if passage had been granted to another world. Fortunately, as Gates later recalled, integration in the Piedmont schools was relatively calm. The town officials, unlike those in other Southern states, moved quickly to comply with the Supreme Court ruling. In fact, for many years, the schools remained the only integrated institutions in the town. Unfortunately, the decision to integrate came at the expense of

Howard High School, the town's African American high school. Because Piedmont could not afford to support two high schools, the town council voted to close Howard, a decision that angered many alumni and students. As Gates later wrote in his memoir, the blacks in Piedmont were tremendously supportive of the school. Everybody liked everything from the building to the basketball team to the school's sense of identity and pride. However, what would not be missed were the worn-out and outdated textbooks.[1]

So it was that in 1956, Henry Jr. entered the Davis Free Elementary School, located at the top of Kenny House Hill. Founded in 1906, the school was a three-story red brick building; it housed grades 1 through 6. Approximately 250 students attended Davis Free Elementary. It was an exciting time, but a frightening one as well. Not everyone accepted the end of legal segregation. Some students who had begun their education at Davis Free when it was segregated resented sharing their school with blacks.

Almost immediately, a new set of rules was put into place to avoid potentially embarrassing or racially charged situations. This included rules that barred interracial dating, dancing, or any show of affection between blacks and whites. There were also rules regarding sports: the number of black players in the starting line-up of the football team was limited; there could be only one black cheerleader. No matter how talented or intelligent, most of the black students were relegated to the "B" track, which consisted mainly of vocational courses such as metalworking, carpentry, or auto repair. These courses were considered not as academically challenging. In case any of the rules were broken, corporal or physical punishment was the result. As Gates later recounted, going to the white school was fine as long as the black students obeyed the rules.[2]

"WHITE SCHOOL"

"In the newly integrated school system, race was like an item of apparel that fitted us all up tight," wrote Gates in his memoir many years later. Everyone in the black community of Piedmont, while excited about the changes, was also frightened and concerned that the transition would not go smoothly and without incident. Every day when Henry

Jr. returned home, Pauline would be waiting for him, asking him and Rocky questions about their school day, what they learned, how they were treated, what people said to them, and, more important, the tone they used when talking to her boys. "Mama did not play when it came to her boys," Gates recalled, "and she wasn't going to let any white woman or man step on her babies' dreams."[3]

Almost from the beginning, Henry Jr. (or Louis, as he was called at school) felt at home with education. From his first day in first grade, he was singled out to excel in his studies. In part, this early recognition was due to his initial test scores, which showed him to be an uncommonly intelligent and thoughtful child. He was also, by his own account, smart, blessed with a good memory, and ample self-confidence. His drive to succeed was also spurred by his older brother Rocky's outstanding scholastic work. Young Henry had the will, the intelligence, and the perseverance to succeed. His teachers encouraged him in his studies, with the exception of his first-grade teacher, who accused him of stealing her scissors. Her accusations only drove Henry Jr. to study harder. His efforts paid off; he earned all As in her class for the rest of the school year.

By the time he entered second grade, Henry Jr. had emerged as one of the shining stars at Davis Free Elementary School. He often wore a white cotton sweatshirt with a chessboard on the front that he considered his "personal coat of arms." On a standardized test, he scored 489 correct answers out of a possible 500. His test results throughout school continued to be so outstanding that his teachers personally came to his house to tell his proud parents.[4]

By the fourth grade, Henry Jr. had met his "soul mate," a white girl by the name of Linda Hoffman. Together, they were the two smartest students in their classes. They exchanged pictures. On Valentine's Day, when the students exchanged cards in their brown bag "mailboxes," Henry and Linda always made each other an extra card. Henry Jr. was so taken with her that he would often walk a half a mile out of his way to go by her house in the hope of seeing her. Unfortunately, the complications of race were always in the background. They came to a head when a traveling magician performed his act for the students at Davis Elementary. At one point, he asked Linda to pick out her boyfriend, who would come on stage with her for his next trick. Gates remembers hearing the words "I want Skippy" ring through the auditorium. The audience nervously laughed as Henry Jr. walked onstage. Flustered, the magician sped through his trick and quickly hustled the two children off the stage. Henry Jr., proud to be chosen, was also angered by the response of his classmates and the adults. It was another not-so-subtle reminder that even though legal segregation had been abolished in the schools, the idea of "separate and not necessarily equal" still had a strong hold on the community in Piedmont.[5]

There were other, more painful and poignant reminders of the racism that simmered beneath the surface of everyday interactions between whites and blacks. Rocky Gates often bore the brunt of his teachers' racist attitudes. Once, when competing for a literary prize, he was told that he did not have to practice. Instead, Pauline worked with Rocky night after night on his recitation, "The Creation," written by African American poet James Weldon Johnson. Not only did Rocky deliver a powerful performance, he won the competition, much to the chagrin of the white teacher who had told him he did not need to practice. It turned out that she had wanted a white student to win the award.

Another episode scarred Rocky Gates even more deeply. In the eighth grade, Rocky was in competition for a Golden Horseshoe, a prize given for excellence in state history. It was among the highest academic honors that could be won in West Virginia. There were four winners chosen from each county, who then traveled to the state capital in Charleston and met the governor. Rocky was acknowledged to have been in contention; if he won, he would be the first African American student in the state to take home the coveted award. Rocky was told that he had missed winning by half a point because of a misspelling. He was devastated that he had come so close, only to lose because of a misspelled word. The truth later emerged when a white friend of Henry Sr.'s came to the house one night and told the Gateses that Rocky did not win because he was black. He had not made a spelling mistake. Rather, the Charleston hotel where the winners and their families always stayed was segregated. A black family would not have been allowed to stay, and so Rocky was passed over for the award.[6]

It was up to Pauline to break the news to Rocky that the county school board had lied to him. And although Rocky was relieved to know that he had not made a mistake, the knowledge that he had been denied the award because of his color was a devastating blow. Henry Jr. wrote much later that it seemed as if his brother's childhood had died the day he heard the news. The event troubled Rocky for most of his life. Henry Jr. learned the lesson, too. It did not stop him from winning the award six years later. Rocky continued to break new ground in school. His achievements, successes, and disappointments helped his younger brother to navigate the shifting and tricky waters of racism. Henry Jr. was grateful for his brother's courage and determination; it made his path a little easier when it came time for him to follow in his brother's footsteps.[7]

The integration of the Piedmont schools also brought an unexpected benefit to the Gates household. In 1957, Pauline Gates was elected secretary of the Piedmont School PTA. She was the first African American to hold that, or any, position in the organization. On PTA meeting nights, Henry Jr. dressed up after finishing his dinner and walked with his mother to the town high school. He always sat near the front so he got a good view of the proceedings, but particularly to watch his mother. After being introduced by the PTA president, Pauline Gates would stand and read the minutes of the previous meeting. For her youngest son, listening to her melodic voice was "pure poetry." Her voice was strong, her diction impeccable, her demeanor confident. Her son was always proud to be seen with his mother at these meetings.[8]

Pauline Gates's election to the PTA also opened the way for other blacks in the community to step forward and join the organization, too. She was a leader and a trailblazer, a path that, in their own ways, her sons followed. For many blacks in Piedmont, Pauline Gates was a proud symbol of their community. Many people came to the meetings simply to show their support and their pride at her accomplishments. Like other blacks who enjoyed success, the experience was not singular; every success, like every disappointment, was shared by all.

FATHER AND SON

Henry Jr.'s relationship with his father was at first not as warm or close as his relationship with his mother. In fact, he believed that his father preferred Rocky's company to his. Unlike Henry Jr., who struggled with his weight, Rocky possessed an athlete's body and, in looks, favored his father. The two especially enjoyed watching and playing sports, particularly baseball, where Henry Jr. was content to watch rather than participate. But not always. When taken to a baseball game in Pittsburgh, where he watched two of the greatest pitchers in the National League—Don Drysdale and Sandy Koufax of the Los Angeles Dodgers—all Henry Jr. could think of was how he wanted to go home. Years later, he would laughingly recall how the most "boring night of my life" was actually one of the greatest as he had the opportunity to see two of baseball's greatest pitchers play in the same game. But Henry Jr. did like traveling to the games; not only did it offer an opportunity to study geography, it also meant eating out at special places such as Howard Johnson's. Still, relations between Henry Sr. and his youngest were often tense and miserable. Henry Sr. was often critical of his youngest son's athletic abilities and would often embarrass Henry Jr. by correcting him or criticizing him in front of strangers.[9]

Yet Henry Jr. did not entirely forsake the baseball diamond. He did play one game in the local Little League baseball as a catcher, a decision made in part because his stout build reminded the coach of another baseball great, Roy Campanella. Henry Jr. soon found himself wearing a chest protector and a facemask and was told to squat and take his position behind the batter. Henry Jr., for his part, was ill suited to the position and the sport. During his first game, he kept closing his eyes, scared to death that the ball would hit him on the head. His one time at bat, he walked. Still, the high point of the day was when he and his father stopped at the Cut-Rate to get a caramel ice cream cone and walk home. As they made their way back to the house, Henry Sr. told his son that he did not have to play ball if he did not want to. He explained to him that when he was a boy, he was not a good player either and was, in fact, afraid of the ball. Instead, he became manager of the team. Henry Jr. took the hint; he turned in his uniform and went on to become the batboy for the team and, later, keep the game statistics for the league.[10]

That incident was a turning point for both father and son. From that day on, Gates remembered years later, relations between the two changed for the better. Although Henry Jr. never embraced or excelled at sports the way his brother did, he did come to appreciate the time spent with his father and Rocky as something to be savored and shared. And over time, the relationship between the two would grow into something that was treasured by both father and son.

AFRICAN DISCOVERIES

By the time Henry Jr. had entered sixth grade in1960, he was an accomplished student and was considered at the top of his class. He was already pondering a career in law or medicine. Among his favorite subjects was geography. He especially enjoyed studying the globe and world maps to learn about new and exotic places. One of the highlights of the school week was when the class would receive large colored maps; each map would be marked to coincide with a current-affair article that was printed at the bottom of the page. "I lived for that map each week," he later recalled.[11]

One area of the world he found especially fascinating was Africa. During the early 1960s, many of the African nations were breaking away from European colonial powers, such as Portugal, France, and Great Britain, to establish their independence. News stories were filled with accounts of the various independence movements taking place in countries such as Mozambique, Algeria, Angola, and Kenya. Henry Jr. followed the stories carefully both in the newspapers and on television. He made careful notes of the new names he was hearing such as Moise Tshombe, Kwame Nkrumah, and Jomo Kenyatta, all heads of the newly formed African states. Little did he realize that this early fascination with Africa helped plant the seeds for his future travels and writings when he became an adult.[12]

Another favorite subject was history. But the only problem with studying the past, for Gates, was when the discussion turned to slavery. Although the treatment of slavery was brief, it was uncomfortable for Gates and other black students. Listening to descriptions of how African slaves were little more than savages until whites taught them how to be civilized was a source of humiliation and anger. Most of the black students knew better but would not have dared to correct their white teachers. Another, even more troubling message was also hinted at: anytime whites tried to help blacks, they were hurt or killed, such as the abolitionist John Brown and President Abraham Lincoln, who had emancipated the slaves. Henry Jr.'s reaction was mixed with both sadness and anger at the implications that whites had paid the ultimate price for trying to aid blacks.

A GROWING AWARENESS

Despite the promise of equality and better treatment that integration represented, in many ways, the divisions and distance between whites and blacks appeared to be even more pronounced. Although Henry Jr. made many friends, both white and black, there were telling differences in his relationships with the members of each group. White friends would visit his house, but they never stayed for dinner or for an overnight. When Henry Jr. visited white friends, the same limitations applied. In some instances, he was not allowed to enter a white family's dwelling because a friend's parent did not like black people. Black friends, by contrast, often ate dinner at the Gates's house or slept there overnight. It was as if the two worlds could only interact so much before whites and blacks retreated into the safety of their own cultures and environments.

Henry Jr. also began to notice how blacks' attitudes toward their own people were conflicted. His father often had harsh words about the behavior of other blacks. Many of his attitudes were formed when he was in the army and sent to Fort Lee, New Jersey, during the Second World War. There his father came into contact with African Americans from throughout the United States. He observed first hand different customs, sayings, and stories that were all part of the larger African American culture. He admired black men and women who had bettered themselves but had little use for those who perpetuated the worst racial stereotypes of black people. Henry Sr.'s father was even more critical, stating at times that the government should lock up all black people on a large reservation and take care of them, since most clearly could not care for themselves.[13]

One striking difference between father and son was their attitudes toward white people. For the most part, Henry Sr. interacted with whites only when necessary but did not go out of his way to attract their attention or to befriend them. Doing so, he knew, could be inviting trouble on a number of levels. But his youngest son was not so hesitant either to draw close to whites or to criticize them. When he was 10 years old, for example, Henry Jr. took to task a white man, named Mr. Price, who was rude to a Mr. Fisher, an older black man, at a Little League baseball game. Unable to control his anger, Henry Jr., without thinking of the potential consequences, spoke angrily to Mr. Price, telling him to leave Mr. Fisher alone. The crowd fell silent watching the young black boy arguing with the older white man. Henry Sr. stood silent watching the two, though he at last intervened and walked his son away from Mr. Price. He took Henry Jr. over to the area where the black men gathered to watch the game. On their way back home, his father did not chastise his son for his actions but did remind him that trouble invariably arose when blacks talked back to whites.[14]

Perhaps though the most dramatic revelation of his parents' attitudes toward whites came in 1959 while Henry Jr. was watching with his mother the documentary *The Hate That Hate Produced* on television. The film confirmed for Gates the sense of injustice and outrage that blacks felt toward whites. He saw also that there was an alternative to the accommodating behavior he often witnessed from blacks in Piedmont.

The documentary focused on the Nation of Islam, an African American religious organization founded in 1930 in Detroit, Michigan. A traveling peddler, Wallace D. Fard (c. 1877–1934), gathered followers among the poverty-stricken African Americans. Fard mysteriously disappeared in June 1934; he was later identified as an incarnation of Allah. One of Fard's first converts was a man named Elijah Poole, who adopted the name Elijah Muhammad (1897–1975) when he joined the Nation of Islam. When Fard disappeared, it was Elijah Muhammad who assumed leadership of the movement and carried the prophet's message throughout the country. Under Elijah Muhammad and, with the aid of his most able lieutenant Malcolm X (born Malcolm Little, 1925–1965), the Nation of Islam became influential in national and international affairs.[15]

Among the basic tenets of the group is the restoration of the spiritual, social, and economic status of African Americans, who once dominated whites. The Nation of Islam also believes that God will bring universal peace. In addition, the group stressed such individual practices as cleanliness, good manners, responsibility, and respect for all black brothers and sisters. Family is considered to be the foundation of society, and great care must be taken in raising children to reflect both good morals and sound education. Members of the Nation of Islam abstain from drinking alcohol or using drugs or tobacco and emphasize healthy nutrition. Women are respected but subservient to men; they observe a code of modest dress that prohibits the wearing of tight or suggestive clothing and includes wearing the traditional head coverings and applying no makeup.[16]

The Nation of Islam also holds controversial views about race and race relations. Following the pronouncements of Wallace Fard, Elijah Muhammad taught that blacks were descendants of the Shabazz, an ancient African tribe that originally settled Mecca, the holiest city of Islam and the spiritual of the Muslim faith. Elijah Muhammad also insisted that the first human being was a black man who appeared more than 76 trillion years ago. This first man took the name of Allah, or God, and created others in his image. Therefore, all African Americans were the direct creations of and the direct descendants from Allah himself. According to the Nation of Islam, the white man's origins were more malevolent. A mad scientist named Yacub created a race of evil white devils, who have since become the scourge of all living things. At some point, according to the teachings of the Nation of Islam, the reign of the "white devils" would end, the "Black Man's" rule would recover his original power, and the reign of peace and harmony would begin.[17]

Because blacks and whites can share no real community, it is essential that blacks take care of themselves and each other and pursue their own political, economic, and spiritual development. Integration was a sham. According to this theory, blacks must permanently separate themselves from whites, as outlined in one of the basic tenets in the Nation of Islam's doctrine:

> 9. WE BELIEVE that the offer of integration is hypocritical and is made by those who are trying to deceive the Black peoples into believing that their 400-year-old open enemies of freedom, justice, and equality are, all of a sudden, their friends.

> Furthermore, we believe that such deception is intended to prevent Black people from realizing that the time in history has arrived for the separation from the whites of this nation.[18]

While viewing *The Hate That Hate Produced*, Gates saw a side of his mother he never knew existed, as he described in a 1994 interview:

> Malcolm X was talking about the white man was the devil and standing up in white people's faces and telling them off. It was great. I mean, it's what black people did behind closed doors . . . I couldn't believe it. . . . I glanced over at Mama and her face was radiant. I mean, this smile—beatific smile started to transform her face. And she said quite quietly, "Amen." And then she said, "All right now," and she sat up and she said, "Yes." And she loved Malcolm X and she loved what the Muslims were doing. It was like . . . it was like watching the Wicked Witch of the West emerge out of the transforming features of Dorothy. This person I had thought of as this pioneer of the civil rights movement really had a hard time with white people.[19]

Gates subsequently learned that his mother had experienced a number of painful incidents of white racism, especially when she had worked as a servant in the home of a wealthy white family. (Eventually, Gates and his brother would buy the house of that white family for their mother to live in.) Those experiences had taught her never to trust white people, nor did they give her much reason to like or admire them. Despite her own feelings, she realized the importance of integration. As Gates came to understand, his mother wanted him and his brother to live and work in an integrated society, to have the same kinds of opportunities as white people enjoyed. It was the only way she knew for them to be truly successful. Yet no matter how much success her sons might have, the most important thing in the world for Pauline Gates was for them never to forget where they came from or who they were, and not to think that white people could ever be trusted.[20]

There were other signs, too, that race was still at the heart of everything in Henry Jr.'s life. By the time he was in seventh grade, his dreams of being more than a friend to Linda Hoffman were dashed completely. It was as if the two realized that being more than friends was an impossibility given the racial climate of the times. Nothing was ever said, as Gates wrote later, but the words did not have to be spoken, they just understood. Widening the gap between the two friends even further was the decision to move Henry Jr. ahead to eighth grade-level mathematics classes. Not wanting to leave his friend behind, he argued with the teacher that Linda was also as bright and should be moved ahead as well. But he could not change the teacher's decision. From that point on, Henry Jr. was on the fast track in many of his mathematics classes. Even though he and Linda continued to take other classes together, the connection they had once enjoyed was forever broken.[21]

Still, the two continued to talk, often on the phone. As Linda was a voracious reader, Henry Jr. took to reading more and more in an effort to keep up with her. Instead of reading books on sports, he found himself mesmerized by such classic works as *A Tale of Two Cities* and *Les Miserables*, as well as devouring biographies of all types. He often went to the bigger library in Keyser on Saturdays and checked out recordings of the works of Shakespeare and listened to them as he read the plays. He was especially keen on the British actor Richard Burton, whose magnificent speaking voice brought Shakespeare's characters to life.[22]

He found time for other activities as well. He visited one of his uncles frequently to listen to records and learned about jazz and rhythm and blues. He especially enjoyed listening to songs by popular black singers such as Johnny Mathis and Nat King Cole. His uncle also passed on advice on how to treat women to which Henry Jr. listened, hoping against hope that one day he would be able to use his uncle's advice.[23]

In the midst of all this activity, Henry Jr. pursued what had become an ongoing quest to find a girlfriend. He even took up bowling and joined a league in Keyser in an attempt to impress a pretty African American girl, Jeannie Hollingsworth. Every Saturday, he would hitchhike the five miles to the bowling alley to be near her. When she failed to respond, he tried winning the hearts of other girls. He would write out careful scripts to use when he called girls on the telephone. He also considered taping little notes under pillows or furniture with various topics of conversation if they ever visited his home so the conversation would never falter. But his efforts were in vain. His many attempts at romance ended with the object of his desire viewing him more like a brother than a boyfriend. As Gates later joked, he already had one sibling, he did not need or want any more.[24]

NOTES

1. Henry Louis Gates, *Colored People* (New York: Vintage Books, 1995), 91–92.
2. Ibid., 96.
3. Ibid., 96.
4. Ibid., 96.
5. Ibid., 96.
6. Ibid., 98.
7. Ibid., 98–99.
8. Ibid., 33.
9. Ibid., 78–79.
10. Ibid., 82–83.
11. Ibid., 101.
12. Ibid., 101.
13. Ibid., 85.
14. Ibid., 85–87.
15. Nation of Islam, "A Brief History of the Nation of Islam," http://www.noi.org/history_of_noi.htm.
16. Ibid.
17. Beliefnet, "Nation of Islam," http://www.beliefnet.com/Faiths/Nation-of-Islam/index.aspx.
18. Nation of Islam, "What The Muslims Believe," http://www.noi.org/muslim_program.htm.
19. "Booknotes: Colored People by Henry Louis Gates, Jr.," October 9, 1994, http://www.booknotes.org/Watch/60633-1/Henry+Louis+Gates.aspx
20. Ibid.
21. Gates, *Colored People*, 106–107.
22. Ibid., 106–107.
23. Ibid., 106–107.
24. Ibid., 106–109.

Chapter 3

DIRECTIONS TO DESTINY

By 1962, when Gates was 12, life had fallen into predictable and comforting rhythms. Henry Jr. and Rocky were doing well in school. Although not athletic like his brother, Gates had distinguished himself in academic pursuits. Still not as successful with girls as he would like, he was nonetheless popular among his classmates and had many friends. And if political chance continued to sweep the country as African Americans fought for civil and political equality, life in Piedmont and the Gates household were comparatively sedate.

Even though Gates had been regularly attending church, religion took on a deeper meaning for him in 1962. He began noticing that his mother was not quite herself. The woman who had once seemed unafraid of anything that life threw her way became suddenly fearful. Where she had once been the picture of health, she began to gain weight. The house that she had kept so meticulously clean became cluttered. She bought canned goods obsessively as if stocking up for some future catastrophe; she also began hoarding bolts of fabric that soon filled galvanized metal garbage cans. She cried for hours and talked of dying, warning her youngest son to be brave and to prepare himself for her death.[1]

Her actions left Gates baffled and frightened. He tried to ease her burden by helping with the cleaning and the cooking, and even tried his hand at ironing the clothes. No matter what he did to cheer his mother and raise her spirits, he failed. Then he began to read the pamphlets explaining menopause that appeared in the house with titles such as "The Phases of Eve," or "The Change of Life," hoping to figure out what had caused his mother's transformation. Yet understanding left him helpless; he could only watch as his mother grew more depressed each day. Although the cause of her depression was menopause related, the roots of the disorder went much deeper. She never fully recovered. For Gates, his mother's illness was devastating, made the more so by his belief that he had somehow caused it. In time, Pauline Gates's depression worsened so dramatically that she was finally hospitalized.[2]

One Sunday, Gates's mother complained of feeling unwell and believed she was going to die. It was as if the entire family was waiting for something disastrous to happen. Finally, Pauline, with tears in her eyes, pulled her youngest aside and told him that she needed to go to the hospital. She did not know when she would be back, or even if she would be back. She kissed him and left.[3]

Pauline Gates was in the hospital for less than a week and came home with a number of prescriptions. Her condition improved. But, despite her physical recovery, she never regained that vital spark that had made her such a compelling personality. If anything, her depression began to manifest itself in odd and unusual ways throughout the coming years. She became fearful of objects resting on a flat surface such as a tabletop or countertop, believing that they could fall off. To make sure this did not happen, Pauline continually walked around the house pushing objects back from the edge to calm her obsession. Even though Gates tried to reason with her, it did not change her behavior.[4]

His mother's condition deeply troubled Gates, perhaps more than it should have. For a long time, he believed himself responsible for her illness. Gates had developed a number of his own obsessive behaviors, which he called "rituals," that he held to rigidly. For instance, he would only walk around the kitchen table from right to left. Whenever he passed before it, he never failed to nod his head at the large oak crucifix that his mother had hung in the hallway. Every day, he slept and got out of the bed on the same side. He also always crossed his legs with his right calf over his left. On the Sunday that his mother went to the hospital, Gates decided to reverse his "rituals" and to do the exact opposite of what he had been doing. Writing about the experience years later, Gates was still not quite sure what compelled him to take such actions, though he admitted it might have been out of anger or defiance. If he had not abandoned his "rituals," he reasoned, then his mother would not have fallen ill and would not have had to enter the hospital. Her depression was thus his fault, he thought, and he sought ways to rectify the situation and alleviate the guilt he was feeling. On the Sunday that his mother went to the hospital, Gates made a promise to God: if God spared his mother's life, then he would join the church and devote his life to God. He prayed all day and night, and when his mother lived, he believed that the Lord had answered his prayers.[5]

COMING TO JESUS

When Henry Jr. announced he was joining the local Methodist church, his parents' reaction was mixed. His father could not understand why he wanted to become a member of the church, while his mother, still not feeling well, was more encouraging. Despite his reservations, Gates's father told his son that if he were going to commit to a church, he should do so with all his heart and not be a quitter. Gates's decision once more marked him as a young man who followed his heart; unlike most other teenagers who saw going to church as a tedious exercise, Gates viewed his commitment as honoring his bargain with God.[6]

And so it was on a Sunday afternoon while attending services at the Walden African American Methodist church in Keyser that Gates stood up and walked to the front of the church and proclaimed his conversion and willingness to commit himself to church membership. Gates's appearance caused a disruption in the proceedings; apparently it had been so long since someone had come forward to join the church that the minister was caught off-guard. A few minutes passed before he found the proper passages in the Methodist Book of Rites with which he then formally invited Gates to the congregation. Gates was so overcome by the emotion of the ceremony he cried before taking his seat.

After the service, he stood at the front of the church while a number of the members greeted him, each offering their congratulations with a hug or a handshake. To demonstrate his newfound religious commitment, Gates went to a local dime store. Years before, when he was six years old, he had stolen a box of crayons. That day, making his way to the school-supplies area, he quietly placed the sum of $1.18 near a stack of crayon boxes as an act of atonement for his earlier sin.[7]

He also tried to be more helpful and considerate at home. He began cooking most of the evening meals for his family when his mother was not up to the task. On the days she did cook, he took over the baking duties, turning out cakes and puddings for the family to enjoy. As he worked alongside his mother, he perused the cookbooks, learning about different foods and spices, many of which were not customarily used in the Gates kitchen. He began to realize yet another subtle form of discrimination against blacks; popular cookbooks were aimed at whites. As he remarked years later, "Betty [Crocker] didn't season with bacon drippings or ham hocks, and she didn't cook the vegetables long enough to suit us."[8]

For the next two years, until he was 14, Gates tried to live a religious life. He did not play cards, stopped going to dances, and no longer listened to rock and roll or rhythm and blues music. He also gave up swearing and gambling. Instead, he went to church as often as possible and read his Bible. The only other place he went was to school. Turning away from many of these activities meant Gates spent a great deal of time alone. But he came to relish the solitude.

Time spent alone prompted Gates to think about all manner of subjects. He pondered religious questions and his mother's illness. Contemplating God and religious mysteries also spared him from having to think much about the current state of the world, which seemed to grow more frightening every day with the onset of the Cuban Missile Crisis, the war in Vietnam, and the continuing racial unrest. Yet for all his dedication, religious conversion brought no relief. If anything, religion gave Gates an even greater burden to bear. He became concerned that, with his swearing and card playing, his father would not go to Heaven. He constantly worried about being called to do something of which he was incapable, that in other words, God would bring him a "bad-news message" that would endanger his or his family's well-being. He grew increasingly afraid of the dark, fearing that an angel would visit him and ask him to carry out some mission to achieve salvation, and that he would fail. He also was frightened of the possibility that he would begin speaking in "tongues" and that under the control of the Holy Spirit, would be commanded to do something that he did not want to do. Finally, Gates began to realize that his faith had been precipitated in large part by his fears: the fear of losing his mother, the fear of sinning so greatly he would be sent to Hell, and the fear of life and its many uncertainties. However painful these musings, Gates remained grateful for the faith that had brought him to a deeper relationship with God.[9]

MORE AWARENESS

In the late summer of 1963, when Gates was 13, his uncle, the Reverend Harry A. Coleman, convinced him to attend his church camp, which was essentially a Methodist retreat for teenagers. The camp was located near Williamsport, West Virginia, not far from where Pauline's mother, "Big Mom," was born. Gates agreed. He remembered that experience with great fondness, recalling the campfires, the singing, and his crush on a pretty girl by the name of Eileen Redman.

It was also during this summer camp experience that Gates began to experience sharp pains in his knee after a raucous touch football game. He figured if he stopped playing, the pain would eventually disappear. It did not. Over-the-counter remedies along with soaking, exercise, and rest also failed to alleviate the problem. Gates then consulted two doctors. The first told him he had pulled a muscle and gave him a cane. The second doctor told him that he had not pulled a muscle but had a torn ligament. His solution was for Gates to use crutches until the injury healed.[10]

By the time school resumed that September, Gates was still on crutches, earning him the nicknames Gimp and Gold Brick from his teachers and friends. One day as he was passing by the school's swimming pool, he experienced a pain so intense he could not walk or move. When he screamed two students immediately came to his aid and carried him to the principal's office. A taxicab was summoned to take Gates to the hospital. Once again, he was diagnosed with a torn ligament in his knee and scheduled for surgery, after which he was to have a walking cast put on his leg. During the pre-operative examination, the surgeon and Gates began talking, and Gates told the doctor about his dream of practicing medicine one day.[11]

The doctor asked Gates a number of questions about the history of science. Did he know, for instance, who invented the process of sterilization? Yes, Gates answered, Joseph Lister. How about who discovered DNA, to which Gates replied Watson and Crick. The discussion went on for several minutes. Gates believed that the doctor, impressed with his knowledge, would offer some words of encouragement to him. Instead, the doctor told him to get up and start to walk. Gates could not and fell to the floor in agony. Neither the doctor nor he realized what had happened: Gates had in fact suffered from a slipped epiphysis, or a separated ball and socket in his hip. By standing and trying to walk, Gates had sheared the joint completely apart. Despite Gates's obvious and extreme pain, the doctor left the room, went out into the corridor where Pauline Gates was waiting, and told her, "there's not a thing wrong with that child. The problem's psychosomatic. Because I know the type, and the thing is, your son's an overachiever." Given the racial assumptions of the time, the doctor, in effect, was saying that Gates was suffering from a physical ailment because he aspired to be something he could never be. He wanted to be a doctor, but that goal was beyond his reach because he was black. The tension between aspiration and reality had created anxiety, which had produced the physical symptoms that Gates manifested. Listening to the doctor's diagnosis, Pauline replied, "Get his clothes, pack his bags—we're going to the University Medical Center," which was located in Morgantown, almost 60 miles away. It was the first time that Gates remembered his mother openly challenging the opinion of a white person.[12]

As thrilled as Henry might have been at his mother's response, he had a more pressing concern on his mind. The University Medical Center was where people went when they were very sick. It was also the place you went when you were going to die. As they traveled to Morgantown, Gates fretted about what he believed would be the final moments of his young life. Instead, he received a proper diagnosis and underwent three operations over the course of the next year.

He endured a long and painful recovery. At one point, he was placed in traction, unable to sit or move.

Throughout his recuperation in the hospital, his mother was there every day, often staying from morning until night. She even took a room in a small hotel in order to minimize the driving back and forth between Piedmont and Morgantown. Her depression also seemed to lift, and she and Gates had spirited conversations that helped keep each other from slipping into their own despair. As Henry watched his mother slowly coming out of her depression, he also found himself letting go of the fearful and restrictive religious fundamentalism he had so feverishly embraced.[13]

Eventually Gates began to walk again. But his recovery had come at a high cost. Although the operations corrected the problem, they also shortened Gates's right leg, forcing him once again to wear orthopedic shoes. Nor did the psychological and emotional wounds easily heal. The attitude of the white surgeon brought Gates face to face with the worst kind of racism, which assumed that because a person was black, his intellectual capabilities were limited and that he did not even deserve to dream.

FATHER SMITH

Besides his mother, one of Gates's frequent visitors while he was in the hospital was an Episcopalian priest, Father Smith, who had just arrived to minister to a congregation in Keyser. Father Smith made the two-hour drive up to see Gates, and the two would have long talks about religion and God. Father Smith assured Gates that it was all right to drink, smoke, play cards, and even, on occasion, to swear. He could still be a good Christian. He could even date girls, something that vastly appealed to Gates, who had never quite given up his search for a girlfriend. During his talks with Father Smith, Gates realized that what he was searching for was a spiritual life that was not restrictive, as the one at Walden Methodist. He wanted to be a religious person, but not a prisoner of faith in God. He later described the feeling that arose from his talks with Father Smith as similar to shedding a once-favorite pair of pants in order to try on others that might fit better.[14]

In addition to conversation, Father Smith also brought Gates books to read. The books covered a wide variety of topics: religion, prayer, catechism, the philosophy and history of the Episcopal Church. One book in particular, *Are You Running With Me Jesus?*, Gates found illuminating: in the book the author, an Episcopal priest, spoke to Jesus as one would to a close friend. It was a relationship with God that Gates would have never encountered while at Walden Methodist. In time, he decided that the God he wanted to honor and worship was one that guided him through life's journeys rather than the all-powerful and punishing deity that seemed to prevail at Walden. As he talked over these and other spiritual matters with Father Smith, Gates also came to appreciate that the priest treated him as an equal, entitled to his own thoughts and opinions. Finally in 1966, when Henry was 16, he joined Father Smith's church in Keyser, to the immense pride of his father, who had himself been raised as an Episcopalian.[15]

TWO WORLDS COLLIDE: PETERKIN AND WATTS

The year before he joined the Episcopal Church, Gates, then 15, was awarded a scholarship to attend Peterkin, an Episcopal church camp in West Virginia. His two-week stay was a revelation: more than 100 teenagers, ranging in age from 15 to 18, attended the camp. Gates likened the camp to a giant human kaleidoscope, where he met teens from a variety of backgrounds. Adhering to a regular daily schedule, the campers rose early, ate breakfast in the dining hall, and then attended a prayer service in the chapel. There were seminars in the morning, followed by lunch. Gates spent most afternoons learning the intricacies of bridge. While playing cards, he and his companions talked about current events, religion, books, and other topics of interest. During one of their many conversations, someone suggested that Gates think about applying to a prep school and possibly college at one of the Ivy League schools such as Harvard or Yale. The prospect of attending college, to say nothing of Harvard or Yale, was startling to Gates. He had never considered such a possibility. Yet, only a week into his stay, Gates's reverie was shattered by news of the race riots at Watts, a poor black section of south-central Los Angeles.[16]

The Watts Riot, which raged for five days during the period August 11 to August 15, 1965, began around 7:00 PM on Wednesday, August 11, when police detained a young African American, Marquette Frye, on suspicion of driving under the influence of alcohol. The arresting officer, Lee W. Minikus, was a white California Highway Patrolman. Marquette failed his sobriety test and was placed under arrest. By 7:23 PM, Marquette's brother and mother had arrived at the scene and were also arrested. In the meantime, a large crowd had begun gathering, and more police were called. By 7:40 PM, the police had left the area, but the crowd remained, visibly tense and angry. Soon the crowd became a mob that stormed and looted shops and businesses, stoned or overturned cars and set them ablaze, and threatened police officers who tried in vain to subdue them.[17]

This initial outburst sparked a large-scale riot centered in the commercial district of Watts. To end the violence, the governor of California, Edmund G. "Pat" Brown, Sr., deployed more than 14,000 California National Guard troops. In an effort to contain the violence, the National Guard established a curfew zone was that encompassed more than 45 miles.[18]

The Watts Riots were the largest and costliest outbreak of urban violence to take place in the United States during the 1960s. By the time calm returned on August 16, 34 persons had died, more than 1,000 others had been injured, and more than 4,000 persons were arrested. The loss of property was staggering. Estimates suggest that the rampage had damaged or destroyed more than $40 million worth of property. Even though California public officials tried to put the blame for the unrest on outside agitators, the official investigation, which Governor Brown initiated, found that the riot was a result of the Watts community's longstanding grievances over its poverty, high unemployment rates, substandard housing, and inadequate schools.[19]

A milkman making his deliveries brought word of the Watts riots to the camp when he handed the head counselor a newspaper that carried stories describing the events. Gates remembered staring at the paper, trying to make sense of what he was reading, while some of the white campers watched for his response. As Gates later wrote, he experienced a strange combination of power and powerlessness as he read and thought about how the actions of the blacks in Watts could affect his life. It was, he said, as if their actions, even though they were strangers and on the other side of the country, had somehow become his responsibility, too. In the end, Gates had conflicting feelings of pride and unease over the events in Watts—pride that blacks had at last stood up for themselves and forced whites to take notice of them and unease about how whites might retaliate.[20]

Later that day, a priest at the camp gave Gates a book to read. The novel, James Baldwin's *Notes of a Native Son*, proved an amazing discovery for Gates. For the first time, he read about the black experience: the pride, the embarrassment, and the anxiety of being black in America. *Notes of a Native Son* was also Gates's introduction to black literature. He could not put the book down, for, if nothing else, it helped him realize how groundbreaking the younger generation of African Americans truly was. Unlike their parents, Gates and his contemporaries had interacted with whites on almost a daily basis. He went to the same schools, and gradually, he shopped in the same stores, ate in the same restaurants, and attended the same summer camps. He went to whites' homes as a friend, not as a domestic or handyman. He was in the position to get to know whites in a way his parents could never have imagined.[21]

Despite the intrusion of such events as the Watts riots on the idyllic world of Peterkin, the remaining week passed quietly for Gates. It was as if everyone in their own way absorbed the news about Watts and then went on with their business. For the rest of the time at the camp, people tried to avoid stereotyping—both blacks and whites—while continuing to engage in lofty debates and heated games of bridge, to eat meals in the dining hall, to gather around the evening bonfires, and to pray together. When it came time to go home, Gates cried at the thought of leaving his new friends. He later wrote that upon his return home, his room, filled with books and records, looked like "Cinderella's hovel" and that somehow he had been taken from a engaging and enlightening world of ideas and books to a place where basketball and baseball scores were the most energetic topics of conversation. Try as he might to explain his adventures, he could see that his friends could not understand why he missed camp so much.[22]

EXETER

Not long after returning from camp, Gates got another chance to leave Piedmont. He applied for entrance to the Phillips Exeter Academy, an exclusive college prep school located in Exeter, New Hampshire. The school, founded in 1791, enjoyed a rich tradition of academic excellence. The school offered Gates the opportunity to pursue his academic interests in a way he had not encountered. After an interview with Jay Rockefeller, a former student at the school, Gates took the entrance exam and passed easily. He was admitted to the school on a full scholarship. Gates said good-bye to his parents in Piedmont and drove with his uncle to New Hampshire to begin the school year.[23]

However, Gates did not last long at the school. Sometime during his first semester he "up and decided" that it was time to head back to Piedmont. The dean of the school could not understand why Gates was so determined to go home. He checked Gates's records, saw that his test scores were perfect and that Gates was earning straight As. He met with Gates and told him there was no reason for him to leave, and further, he had no authority to leave the school campus. For Gates, that was enough. One of his classmates, another African American, told Gates, "Think of yourself. Where is Piedmont, anyway?" Gates replied, "I'll be back," though he was not entirely sure if he meant he would come back to Exeter or to someplace like Exeter. Gates returned home to Piedmont, taking his first plane trip. As he later wrote, "I still don't know for sure why I felt I had to leave; I think that Piedmont was just too far to fall back into, so I decided not to have to fall at all. Homesick for Piedmont, I went back, and soon became homesick for Exeter.[24]

THE FEARSOME FOURSOME

The year 1966 brought about a number of startling changes for African Americans. Although the civil rights movement had made impressive gains, particularly in challenging unconstitutional laws in courts and helping to push through new legislation, racism and segregation persisted. Black Americans still faced great disparities in wages and income, struggled with higher crime rates in their neighborhoods, and endured discrimination in housing, education, and jobs. Young blacks in particular saw the civil rights movement as too cautious and conservative to bring permanent change to American society. Part of the problem, they insisted, was that the civil rights leaders were more concerned about what whites perceived as acceptable than about what blacks themselves wanted and needed.

As a consequence, by the mid-1960s, dissatisfaction with the pace of reform was growing. Despite what whites might believe about the civil rights movement as an instrument of black unity, the reality was that blacks, like any ethnic group, were far from monolithic in their attitudes. A number of individuals and groups, including Malcolm X and the Nation of Islam, believed that blacks would never make progress unless they determined their own fate, separate from white influence and interference.[25]

From this mounting dissension came the slogan "black power." A phrase that had existed since the 1950s, "black power" did not become a watchword of a new African American social and political movement until 1966, when the radical black activist Stokely Carmichael (Kwame Ture) adopted and popularized it. Although not a formal organization, the advent of the Black Power movement marked an important turning point in the history of the civil rights campaign and in black–white relations. Through the Black Power movement, blacks, especially the young, achieved a new sense of racial pride. Black Power emphasized self-improvement through self-help, the notion that only by their own efforts could black people improve their lives and their communities. Whites were hostile, untrustworthy, or ignorant even if well meaning, and would, in any event, never willingly yield power to blacks.

Carmichael and other advocates of black power thus demanded more radical changes in the American political system than the leaders of the mainstream civil rights movement were willing to support. The Black Power movement encouraged blacks to form or join all-black political parties that would establish a true base of power that provided the impetus for change. Instead of aspiring to attain what whites believed blacks should be, blacks should create their own personal identities and their own social, political, and economic agendas that addressed their individual and collective needs. Among the first actions of the new movement was the replacement of the word *Negro* with *black* as the preferred description of African Americans. Many associated *Negro* with the degradation of slavery and subservience.[26]

Although some hailed the Black Power movement as a positive force aimed at helping blacks achieve full equality with whites, others were more critical, seeing it as promoting unnecessary militancy and violence, and thereby, driving a bigger wedge between blacks and whites. In reality, the Black Power movement, like the civil rights movement itself, was a complex organism that appealed to many different people for many different reasons. Its emergence coincided with a period in the history of the United States that brought tremendous social and cultural changes for all Americans.[27]

It was impossible for the teenaged Gates not to feel the impact of the Black Power movement. At 16, he had come to realize that the easy friendships he once enjoyed with his white classmates were beginning to wane. The older everyone got, the less likely they were to interact. His first love, Linda Hoffman, now had a white boyfriend; even their phone conversations had dwindled. Increasingly, Gates saw little reason to pursue friendships with whites. The risks had come to outweigh the rewards and so were hardly worth the effort. Instead, he became one of the founding members of the so-called Fearsome Foursome. The group consisted of Roland Fisher, nicknamed Ben or Fisher, Jerry Price, whose nickname was Soul Moe, Rodney Galloway, known as Swano or Swineo, depending on the mood, and Gates, who was known as Gates, Goops Man, or the Professor. Three of the group played basketball for the school team; Gates kept the statistics.[28]

The four young men did everything together. Riding in a 1959 purple Chrysler Sebring convertible, nicknamed the Soul Mobile, the Fearsome Foursome cruised to Keyser along the Main Street, then over to New Creek to visit the bowling alley or Jimmy's Pizza Shop, then back to Piedmont, where they would cross the bridge and drive over to Westernport and Teen Town. When the evening's activities were done, the four returned to Gates's house on Erin Street, where a tasty meal, a television set, and a good stereo system awaited them.

While at the Gates's house, the boys would listen to Gates's growing collection of jazz records as well as to rhythm and blues and soul music.

Gates had also taken up smoking; although his parents disapproved, they told him that he could smoke, but only in his room.[29]

Gates and his friends saw themselves as a "black cultural consciousness club." The young men read books by a number of different black writers—Eldridge Cleaver, Ralph Ellison, Malcolm X—after which they would engaged in spirited discussions. Gates was also the first black in Piedmont to grow out his hair into an Afro, which he thought a more natural hairstyle for blacks, and was a conscious rejection of the various efforts to straighten out their hair that had been popular among blacks during the 1950s. As such, the style became a potent political symbol of the Black Power movement. For many young blacks it also symbolized a link to their African ancestry. At the same time, Gates and his friends undertook to learn basic phrases of Swahili, an ancient African language, and greeted each other with complicated "soul handshakes."[30]

Not everyone was thrilled with Gates's new direction and interests. His uncle Coleman criticized his hair and deridingly called him Malcolm or Stokely. But to Gates, this was an exciting time to be black. There was an opportunity, he wrote later, to forge a "new communal identity," to learn about African ancestry, and to discover the "unutterable, secret name, and that name was BLACK." Gates and his friends argued with Henry Louis Sr. on the hot topics of the day such as the war in Vietnam, the activities of the Black Panthers, and the accomplishments of the civil rights movement. Gates and his friends sometimes spent the night in his room, talking, laughing, and listening to music until the wee hours. He often bought a copy of the *Washington Post* that he and his friends would eagerly read and discuss. Television offered another source of information about the world outside Piedmont. The boys' growing political awareness led to the first organized school boycott in Piedmont, when they encouraged other black students to stay home from school to watch the funeral of slain civil rights leader Martin Luther King, Jr., since local officials refused to cancel classes.[31]

Clearly, throughout the 1950s and 1960s, Piedmont, the United States, and the world were changing. But it would be many years before Gates really understood why his relatives were so reticent about all that had taken place. Even though they welcomed progress toward a more integrated society, they also saw the passing of something once vibrant and nurturing: the closed community of African Americans with their own institutions, businesses, values, and folkways. With the coming of integration, many of those symbols of that black economy, culture, and way of life disappeared. Integration and equality were necessary and good for blacks. Probably no African American ever longed for a return to the days of segregation and discrimination, legal or otherwise. But as Gates came to appreciate, integration and equality had been purchased at a high and sometimes unexpected price. Much had been gained. At the same time, much that was precious and cherished had been lost. With new freedoms came new responsibilities and new dangers. But for Henry Louis Gates, Jr. at the end of the 1960s, the world seemed full of unmatched possibilities and opportunities to learn and to grow that only a few years earlier had been beyond his reach. As he entered his final year of high school at Piedmont High, the world beckoned. He prepared to answer its call.

NOTES

1. Henry Louis Gates, Jr., *Colored People* (New York: Vintage Books, 1995), 127–128.
2. Ibid., 128.
3. Ibid., 129.
4. Ibid., 129–130.
5. Ibid., 129.
6. Ibid., 130–131.
7. Ibid., 131–133.
8. Ibid., 133.
9. Ibid., 134–135.
10. Ibid., 139.
11. Ibid., 140–141.
12. Ibid., 140–141.
13. Ibid., 141–144.
14. Ibid., 144–145.
15. Ibid., 145–146.
16. Ibid., 147–148.
17. Civil Rights Digital Library, "Watts Riots," http://crdl.usg.edu/events/watts_riots/?Welcome.

18. Ibid.

19. Ibid.

20. Gates, *Colored People*, 149–150.

21. Ibid., 150–151.

22. Ibid., 151.

23. Henry Louis Gates, Jr., "Joining the Black Overclass at Yale University," *The Journal of Blacks in Higher Education*, no. 11 (Spring 1996): 99.

24. Ibid., 99.

25. "Black Power Movement," http://law.jrank.org/pages/4776/Black-Power-Movement.html.

26. Ibid.

27. Ibid.

28. Gates, *Colored People*, 181–182.

29. Ibid., 182.

30. Ibid., 186.

31. Ibid., 186–188.

Chapter 4

A QUEST FOR IDENTITY

In 1968, three of the Fearsome Foursome graduated from Piedmont High School. Gates had the honor of serving as class valedictorian. As before, he continued to break the rules, this time by writing his own speech, even as he practiced the traditional speech given at graduation with his English teacher. He rehearsed his own speech at home with his mother. On graduation day, instead of giving the prepared speech authorized by the school, Gates substituted his address. Whereas the traditional valedictorian address spoke of values and school and sentimental remembrances, Gates's speech explored the pressing issues facing the Class of 1968: the war in Vietnam, the civil rights movement, and women's issues such as equality and abortion. He also reminded the class of the great sense of community they had shared. All in all, the speech appeared to be a success. Even his English teacher was pleased with his performance.[1]

Of his four close friends, one, Soul Moe, was drafted and sent to Vietnam. Roland had been held back in school. Gates and Swano were college bound and in the fall would begin classes at Potomac State College of West Virginia University. The college was located in Keyser, so Henry Louis Jr. would still be close to his family. Although he was relieved to have finished high school, he was excited and a little frightened at the prospect of beginning college. Gates had never thought about attending college anywhere but Potomac. It was understood that once one graduated from Piedmont High School, Potomac was where one went to college. A number of his relatives, including his brother Rocky, had studied at Potomac. After he completed his studies there, he would apply to the University of West Virginia at Morgantown, where he hoped to finish his undergraduate studies and realize his dream of becoming a physician.[2]

CLASSES WITH THE DUKE

In late August 1969, a week before Labor Day, Gates arrived at Potomac State to enroll for his classes. He had been an excellent student all his life but was still unsure and frightened at the possibility that he might not be smart enough to handle college courses. His cousin Greg helped him by talking about what student life was like, about how much he would enjoy his new freedom, and of the women he would meet. He also recommended a teacher for Gates: Duke Anthony Whitmore, who taught English. Gates at first was confused by the name and asked if the professor was an Englishman. No, his cousin laughed, he was a white man from Baltimore who was one of the best teachers on campus.[3]

Not only did Gates take his cousin's advice and register for Whitmore's class, he requested and got Whitmore to serve as his academic advisor. For Gates, becoming one of Whitmore's students was a revelation about how rewarding the study of literature, both English and American, could be. From the first day in Whitmore's class, Gates was hooked on the study of literature. For Gates, who had regarded reading as a pastime but never a vocation, the world suddenly took on a very different appearance. His dream of attending medical school vanished as he began applying himself to the study of literature.[4]

Gates especially liked that Whitmore's classes were not just about reading the classics of American and English literature. They were also a place where students could debate the hot-button issues of the day such as civil rights, racial discrimination, the war, and current events.

In addition, one of Whitmore's favorite exercises was to recite a passage from a poem, play, or novel and ask students to identify the source. For Gates, Whitmore's classes provided an amazing introduction to the world of ideas. He seriously contemplated pursuing an English major.[5]

After Gates had completed his first year at Potomac, Whitmore suggested that he transfer to an Ivy League school such as Harvard or Yale. Gates decided to try for Yale, and before the spring semester ended, had submitted his application. In the meantime, during the summer, he began to work in the personnel office at the paper mill in Piedmont, where he tried to recruit black workers for the craft or skilled positions available in the mill. During the course of the summer, Gates was pleased to see that he had helped in the gradual integration of the labor unions whose members worked in the mill. As skilled workers, blacks were now eligible for membership in the unions, and they could not only make better money but also enjoy the benefits of union membership.[6]

A DANGEROUS LOVE

It was during his first year in college that Gates also experienced his first serious romantic relationship. The young white woman, Maura Gibson, was someone whom he had known from Piedmont High School, but the two did not become close until they began attending Potomac. In the beginning, they enjoyed having long conversations over the phone. Then the couple began going out secretly, often rendezvousing near the African American cemetery in Keyser. By the summer of 1969, Gates was driving to Rehoboth Beach in Delaware, where Maura had a job as a waitress. He would often leave work on Friday afternoon to make the journey, arriving at Rehoboth Beach around midnight. The two met after Maura's shift ended and usually spent the weekend together, eating steamed crabs, drinking beer, and listening to the radio.[7]

As exciting as the relationship was for Gates, it was also dangerous. Many Americans still regarded interracial romance with distaste and hostility. Gates later admitted that in dating Maura, he felt that he was making some sort of political statement. Perhaps such an attitude was unavoidable. As late as 1960, 31 states outlawed interracial marriage, and only in 1967, when interracial marriage was still illegal in 17 states, did the U.S. Supreme Court declare such restrictions unconstitutional. During the late 1960s, more and more Americans were becoming aware of interracial relationships, as, for example, the marriage of popular entertainer Sammy Davis, Jr. to May Britt Wilkins, a Swedish actress, and the popular film, *Guess Who's Coming to Dinner*, in which the daughter of an affluent white couple brings home a black man whom she intends to marry. Even though Gates was by now used to being the only black person in many white settings such as the beach or a restaurant, he was not as aware of the effect he and Maura had on people until one day a man set his dog loose to attack the couple as they were walking.[8]

One evening, Gates came to pick up Maura at a friend's house; the couple had parked at the local cemetery and then Gates dropped his girlfriend near her home and returned to Piedmont. By time he had got home, there were several frantic messages from Maura. It turned out that her father had followed her and had seen her with Gates. When her father learned that she was dating a black man, he was outraged. In no time, everyone in Keyser and Piedmont knew about the couple, who were apparently the first interracial couple in Mineral County. Both Maura and Gates received threats. Some of Gates's friends became so concerned that they told his parents what was happening. His parents responded by buying Henry Louis Jr. a more reliable car so that he could travel in relative safety between Keyser and Piedmont. In the midst of the uproar, Maura's father, 'Bama Gibson, announced his candidacy for mayor of Keyser.[9]

A DANGEROUS EVENING

Despite the trouble that his relationship with Maura had brought, Gates was not deterred from pushing for greater civil rights for blacks. He and the rest of the Fearsome Foursome decided to integrate a local college hangout known as the Swordfish that featured live music on Friday nights. So it was that one Friday when the club was packed with white college students, the four pulled into the parking lot. Although they were afraid, the four young men made their way up the stairs to the club and walked in. Almost instantly, everyone in the club stopped talking and dancing and stared as the four black men made their way through the crowded dance floor. Then from the crowd, someone shouted at Gates and his friends, calling them "niggers." It was as if, Gates later recalled, several of the whites were seeing their worst nightmare come true: a group of black men coming in to talk, dance, and drink in their club, and perhaps to flirt with white women. Slowly a group of young white men formed a circle around the Fearsome Foursome; the air was crackling with hatred and the threat of potential violence. Gates remembers seeing several of his white friends standing there but doing nothing to help him or his friends. Then the owner burst through the crowd, telling Gates and his friends to leave immediately. He also slammed Roland's head against the wall. Grabbing their friend, Gates, Moe, and Swano headed back through the crowd, yelling at the owner that they would see his club shut down. They made it safely to the car and drove back to Piedmont, where Gates's mother treated Roland's head wound. Gates later stated that as a result of his actions that night, he lost a lot of his white friends.[10]

Gates meant every word he said to the owner of the club. The following Monday, he called the State Human Rights Commission. A few days later, the commissioner came to Piedmont, where he interviewed Gates and his friends. The commissioner also went to the Swordfish and talked with the owner, who, in the meantime, had made threats throughout the town that he would get Gates. The owner also told the commissioner that he would close his club down before he would allow blacks on the premises. The owner was then sent a letter from the Commission office stating that unless the Swordfish integrated, the club would be permanently shut down. True to his word, the owner closed the doors to his establishment. In time, the building became a restaurant owned by a Filipino family.[11]

THE CAMPAIGN

At the same time the turmoil over the Swordfish was raging, the mayoral campaign in Keyser was also heating up. Many citizens, upon hearing about 'Bama Gibson's daughter dating a black man, stated they would not vote for him. But others saw an opportunity to show that Keyser was not a backward small town with small-minded people.

Many whites chose to support 'Bama Gibson precisely because his daughter was dating a black man. The black members of the community also decided to support Gibson. As Gates later wrote, it was as if the mayoral race had turned into a referendum on interracial romance. In the end, Gibson, a mailman, won handily over his opponent, the former president of Potomac College.[12]

From that point on, Gates and Maura were left alone. No longer did they have to fear being pulled over by the police and harassed. They still faced racist comments, but overall, the atmosphere of the town had calmed. 'Bama Gibson even went so far as to notify Gates that the West Virginia State Police had created a file on him, identifying him as possible suspect in the event there was ever any racial unrest in the area. Gates did not know whether to be frightened, sick, or flattered that he had gained so much notoriety. But he also realized that it was time for him to leave Piedmont and Keyser. He had gone as far as he could. He knew he wanted more from the world and that as much as he loved his home, staying there would be suffocating. That fall, he left for Yale and the beginning of a journey that would take him across the ocean to Africa.[13]

YALE

In his personal statement included with his application to Yale University, Gates wrote, "My grandfather was colored, my father was Negro, and I am black . . . As always, whitey now sits in judgment of me, preparing to cast my fate. It is your decision either to let me blow with the wind as a non-entity or to encourage the development of self. Allow me to prove myself."[14]

Much to his surprise, the Yale office of admissions decided to take a chance on Gates. That fall, he traveled to New Haven, Connecticut, to begin his studies "with the blackest class in the history of that ivy-draped institution."[15] Gates wrote later about his decision to attend Yale:

> I picked Yale almost out of a hat. After a year at a junior college near my home, a place where "nigger" was hung on me so many times that I thought it was my name, I decided to head north,

armed with a scholarship and a first edition of Strunk and White's *The Elements of Style*."[16]

Describing his first impressions of the college, Gates wrote in 1996:

> By day—and it was still light when I first arrived in New Haven—the university is a tangible, mortar-and-stone manifestation of an Oxonian ideal of Gothic perfection. By night, the sense of enchantment increased: the mammoth structures, strangely out of keeping with the surrounding town, guarded their streets with bearded shadows made by the half-light of the lampposts. At Yale, battle hymns were Congregational, with delicate changes of key. The building that just had to be the college cathedral turned out to be Sterling Library. Every feature of the place was alarming and exhilarating. Welcome to Never-Never Land, I told myself. This is your world, the world you've longed for and dreamed of. This was where the goods and entitlements of the American century were stored and distributed. It was the grown-up version of the world of Captain Midnight Decoders; the repository of all those box tops I used to ship off to Kellogg's in fair exchange for laser guns.[17]

It was a heady experience for Gates and for Yale. In 1970, the university accepted 95 African American students, the first of what was regarded as the "affirmative action generation," admitted not only for their abilities but also in an attempt to increase the number of minority students on campus. Many of the black students at Yale were the first in their families to attend college. Other students were the sons and daughters of wealthy, old "colored money." In a 2010 interview, Gates reflected on his time at Yale:

> I loved Yale. We [he and the other black students] were on the great adventure of black discovery. We were discovering ourselves as future leaders in the largest numbers up to that time at a university of that caliber. We were in a position of privilege, and we recognized our historical responsibility. We knew how lucky we were. Yale's class of '66 had six African-Americans in it.

> The class of '70 had 96. Yale's affirmative action was about the dismantling of racist historical quotas. Yale was very explicit about the fact that we were part of the 1,000 male leaders they produced (and 250 female leaders).[18]

STUDYING THE AFRICAN AMERICAN

Gates's arrival at Yale coincided with the introduction of a new academic discipline to the curriculum: Afro-American studies. The idea of an academic discipline focusing on African American life, history, and culture was not new; the annual Atlanta University Conferences held between 1898 and 1914, under the direction of noted African American writer and activist W. E. B. Du Bois, had marked the first organized study of the African American experience, focusing on such aspects as health, economic development, the church, politics, and culture. It was also during this period that African American studies were formally introduced into an academic context by African American educators and academics.[19]

One of the most important goals that the black intellectuals of this earlier period had hoped to achieve was to diminish and, in time, to eradicate the many negative representations and stereotypes of blacks in American society and culture. During this period, the accepted historical and social scientific research suggested that blacks were genetically inferior to whites and, further, that Africa itself was little more than a wild and untamed jungle populated by peoples scarcely a generation removed from cannibalism. To counteract these vicious studies and prejudices, the American Negro Academy, established in 1896, had set as one of its major goals to document through research and publication the truth about Africa and African Americans. Through careful scholarship, members of the Academy hoped to vindicate their race.[20]

In 1915, the historian and writer Carter G. Woodson established the Association for the Study of Negro Life and History (ASNLH), marking the first appearance of an established African American studies program. The purpose of the ASNLH was lofty but straightforward: to promote historical research; to publish books on black life and history; and to encourage the study of African American culture through clubs and schools. The organization also stressed its desire to promote racial harmonies. A year later, in 1916, Woodson founded the *Journal of Negro History*, serving as its editor until his death in 1950. The journal is still in publication and remains one of the most important and influential academic journals for the study of African American history and culture. But Woodson's most important contribution came in 1926 when, with the aid of several his colleagues, he created Negro History Week, a time in which the study of African American history and the accomplishments of African American culture would be celebrated. In 1976, 50 years after Woodson had announced a week-long commemoration of African American history, the week expanded to encompass the entire month of February, becoming Black History Month, as it is known today. In response to Woodson's revolutionary gesture, historically black colleges and universities began incorporating black studies courses into their curriculums.[21]

The period between approximately 1940 to the mid-1960s marked yet another era in the study of African American history and life characterized by a growing legitimacy and an increasing number of white scholars who now engaged in such research. Prior to this time, black scholars had carried out the vast majority of the research conducted on African Americans. By the 1960s, the field, now known alternately as African American Studies, Africana Studies, Afro-American Studies, Black Studies, and Pan-African Studies, was becoming more integrated. The discipline was given a further boost by the growing social unrest that accompanied the civil rights, Black Power, and African liberation movements that had emerged during the 1950s and 1960s. This growing political and social awareness had instilled in the growing number of black faculty members and students a need for classes that addressed the history and social problems of African Americans.

As a result, a number of African American organizations began appearing on campuses throughout the United States to demand changes in the traditional college curricula, including courses on black history, culture, and other aspects of black life. The purpose of this field of study was not only to improve the conditions under which black people lived but also to enhance their self-image and self-esteem and build their sense of identity and character. In some cases, black students began to refuse to take traditional American or Western European courses that stressed the achievements of white men.[22]

By the late 1960s, the first African American Studies programs were established at San Francisco State College (now University), Merritt College in Oakland, California, and Cornell University in Ithaca, New York. In 1968, San Francisco State established the first African American Studies department. In 1969, Cornell University followed suit with the establishment of an African Studies and Research Center. Initially rooted in the study of history, sociology, literature, and the arts, African American studies offered a radical departure from prevailing academic practices and traditions in its call for a multicultural interpretation of the Western Hemisphere rather than the traditional Eurocentric one that had been in place for decades and that had either denigrated or ignored Africans and their descendants.[23]

A NEW AWARENESS

Gates's experiences at Yale were heady, exciting, and enlightening. His arrival on campus, coinciding with the emergence and heightened awareness of African American studies and the Black Power movement, added a dimension to his education and his life that he would have never had if he had stayed in Piedmont and gone on to the University of West Virginia. Gates recalled that as a member of that large entrance class of African Americans at Yale, he was among a "fledging elite" or a "vanguard" that took its responsibilities very seriously. At once afraid of faltering under the stringent academic requirements but excited about the prospects for personal and social growth and change made for memorable conversations and get-togethers. Not only did Gates and his black classmates have the opportunity to study at Yale, they were also going to integrate the school's most exclusive societies, clubs, and organizations. If all went well, they would graduate with degrees that promised to open the door to even further advancement in the real world. One day, they might even find themselves with the power to make their voices heard, to speak for their people, and to effect positive change.

Even though black faces among the faculty were few, there were dozens of role models for Gates and his cohorts to follow. As Gates recalled, many of the students took at least one course in the new program in Afro-American studies, in part out of a "sense of team spirit," and partly to just learn more about themselves and their history and culture. Gates took several courses in the department and "at least three times found myself assigned to read Du Bois's essay 'The Talented Tenth.'"[24]

For Gates, W. E. B. Du Bois served as a role model throughout his time at Yale. The noted abolitionist Frederick Douglass, the athlete, singer, actor, and civil rights activist Paul Robeson, the lawyer and Supreme Court Justice Thurgood Marshall, and, of course, Dr. Martin Luther King, Jr. were also important sources of inspiration for Gates and his classmates. For those African American students who were more politically radical, such figures as Marcus Garvey, the slave insurrectionist Nat Turner, and the West Indian psychiatrist and writer Frantz Fanon were even more influential.[25]

Not long after his arrival at Yale, Gates attended his first meeting of the Black Student Alliance at Yale. Gates was amazed when many of the students complained about how few blacks there were on the campus. For Gates, looking around at the large number of students in attendance made him feel as if "I were in Africa, or Harlem, anyway." For him, he had never seen so many black people his own age in one place. As he wrote later, "I'd grown up in colored Piedmont; here I would truly learn how to be black." Gates ended up volunteering to act as secretary for the organization, even though he worried, as he told a friend while attending a rally, "I'm not black enough."[26]

ROLE MODELS

There were two students that Gates came to admire during his time on campus: Glenn DeChabert and Armstead Robinson. Gates had first heard of them when he read an article in the pages of the Yale alumni magazine the summer before he arrived at Yale. The article was about the two sophomores who had put together a conference on the Yale campus that focused on the state of Afro-American studies on campuses. For Gates, the two young men embodied ideals that he admired: DeChabert for his leadership skills and Robinson for his scholarship. Of the two, Robinson would become close friends with Gates:

> Thin and ascetic in his unpressed dashiki and uncombed afro, Robinson . . . was the first black "Scholar of the House," part of a competitive senior-year program in which a major scholarly project was pursued instead of regular course work. Robby, we knew, would change the way we understood our past and our present, by dint of his extraordinary and well-stocked mind. Once I gained his friendship, I'd go over to his room at Morse College and sit on the floor cross-legged as he typed away. "I won't bother you," I'd tell him. "I just want to watch you work." The truth is that I was starstruck: I'd never met a black scholar before, and in some almost mystical way I . . . [hoped] that the magic would rub off.[27]

Gates tackled his studies with a vengeance, fearful that he would not make the grade academically. He worked at his studies every day, often until late in the evening. He was convinced he would be nothing more than an average student; all he hoped was to make the grade of C+. Where once he had been eager to speak up in class, he now did so hesitantly. But it would be in History 31 where Gates hit his stride. He worked extra hard in the class; when it was time to prepare his first paper, Gates admitted that:

> Never have I put so much work and expectation, fear and care, into the preparation of a five-page paper. Had the returned grade been a Pass, or just a High Pass, the tenor of my years at Yale would probably have been as gray as a New Haven winter. But there it was, in unforgettable bright red letters: "Honors. Nice Paper." "Honors."

That very night, Gates decided he was going to go to Africa the next year and that one day, he too, would be a Scholar of the House, just like Robinson.[28]

Between his studies and other activities on campus, Gates's first year at Yale raced by. Not only were there classes to study for, but there were also rallies to attend, campus groups to work with, and social events. It was a time, as Gates later wrote, in which "People all of a sudden had to prove that they were black; you had to wear your bona fides. It was as if there were some keeper of blackness who was in a position to say you are black or you are not black." Though in Piedmont Gates had been highly political, at Yale he learned he was not really cut out for the high stakes of political activism. In fact, the Black Panthers who gathered near campus, the "fashion plates of black insurrection," made him uncomfortable and tense. The Panthers spent a good deal of time at Liggett's Drug Store, near the Yale campus, where they sold their newspapers and would solicit funds for their breakfast programs for black children. To ignore them was inviting derisive comments, but Gates did the best he could.[29]

OTHER INSPIRATIONS

Another source of inspiration among the African American students at Yale was the cult film *Putney Swope*, released in 1969. The film is a savagely funny and satirical look at the world of Madison Avenue, long considered the center of American advertising. In the film, Putney Swope, the only black man on the executive board of an advertising firm, is accidentally elected as head of the board after the unexpected death of the chairman. Even though each member of the board believes that he would be a better choice to lead the company, the bylaws of the corporation prohibit voting for oneself. Instead, each white member votes by secret ballot for Swope, whom they believe no other white member would support. This strategy results in his election.

As the board's new director, Swope renames the business Truth and Soul, Inc., and replaces all but one of the white employees. Among Swope's key executive decisions is that the company will no longer accept business from companies that produce alcohol, war toys, or tobacco. The success of the business draws unwanted attention from the U.S. government, which considers it a threat to national security.[30]

For Gates and his classmates, the film offered a counterpoint to what they might accomplish once they left the hallowed halls of Yale. As Gates wrote many years later:

> We were determined not to allow our individual, or collective, success to be "used by the man" to justify the continued economic

> deprivation of all those black souls left behind in America's ghetto. No, we would not be tokens; we would not be sellouts; we would not be complicit in the use of the black people in the ghettos as scapegoats either for American prosperity or—more alarmingly—for our individual success.[31]

Gates was also reminded again that the African American community was not monolithic. Further, he saw that even as black people continued to fight for civil rights, within their own community there were many instances of prejudice, discrimination, and oppression. In an interview, Gates described an incident that took place during his first year at Yale:

> We had this special meeting of the Black Student Alliance to talk to the black men—young black men from New Orleans, some of whom were very light complected. And they wanted to have something called a bag party. So, you know, what's a bag party? They wanted to put this paper bag over the door and anyone who was darker than the paper bag couldn't get into the party. So, you know, I looked at them—I was secretary of the Black Student Alliance—everyone from the North and everyone who had any kind of sense and was not from New Orleans said, "We've never heard of such a thing. You guys can't do this. I mean, this is some sort of antiquated, sick relic of the past. I mean, you can't do that."[32]

Even though the practice was stopped, Gates learned later in his African American history classes that the very practice he decried was an accepted part of African American life in New Orleans. It was one of many experiences that made for an exhilarating, exciting, frightening, and intense first year at a new school in a new city and in a new part of the country. But as Gates learned, his experiences at Yale were only the beginning to unlocking a door of self-discovery and the gateway to an unlikely career that he could have never anticipated.[33]

NOTES

1. Henry Louis Gates, *Colored People* (New York: Vintage Books, 1995), 191.

2. Ibid., 192.
3. Ibid., 192.
4. Ibid., 192–193.
5. Ibid., 193–194.
6. Ibid., 194.
7. Ibid., 195.
8. Ibid., 196.
9. Ibid., 196.
10. Ibid., 198–199.
11. Ibid., 199.
12. Ibid., 200.
13. Ibid., 200–201.
14. Ibid., 201.
15. Henry Louis Gates and Cornel West, *The Future of the Race* (New York: Alfred A. Knopf, 1996), 3.
16. Henry Louis Gates, "Joining the Black Overclass at Yale University," *The Journal of Blacks in Higher Education*, no. 11 (Spring 1996): 95.
17. Gates and West, *The Future of the Race*, 3–4.
18. Raina Kelly, "Blackness 101: Skip Gates Talks about Black History Month—and What It Means to Be Black Today," *Newsweek*, February 7, 2010, http://www.newsweek.com/2010/02/06/blackness-101.html.
19. Darlene Clark Hine, "Black Studies: An Overview." In *Black Studies in the United States: Three Essays*, Darlene Clark Hine, Robert L. Harris, and Nellie McKay, eds. (New York: The Ford Foundation, 1990), 50–58.
20. L. Crouchett, "Early Black Studies Movements." *Journal of Black Studies* 2, no. 2 (1971): 189–200.
21. Clark Hine, "Black Studies: An Overview," 50–58.
22. Vernon J. Williams, Jr., "African American Studies," *Dictionary of American History*, Stanley I. Kutler, ed. 3rd ed. 10 vols. (New York: Charles Scribner's Sons, 2003). Reproduced in History Resource Center. Farmington Hills, MI: Gale. http://galenet.galegroup.com/servlet/HistRC/.
23. Ibid.
24. Henry Louis Gates, Jr., "Joining the Black Overclass at Yale University," *The Journal of Blacks in Higher Education*, no. 11 (Spring 1996): 97.

25. Henry Louis Gates, Jr., *America behind the Color Line: Dialogues with African Americans* (New York: Warner Books, 2004), ix.

26. Gates, Jr., "Joining the Black Overclass at Yale University," 96.

27. Ibid.

28. Ibid., 99.

29. Cheryl Bentsen, "Head Negro in Charge," *Boston Magazine*, July 23, 2009, http://www.bostonmagazine.com/articles/Henry_Louis_Gates_Jr/page3.

30. Film *Putney Swope*. 1969.

31. Gates, Jr., *America behind the Color Line: Dialogues with African Americans*, x–xi.

32. "Booknotes: Colored People by Henry Louis Gates, Jr.," October 9, 1994, http://www.booknotes.org/Watch/60633-1/Henry+Louis+Gates.aspx

33. Ibid.

Chapter 5
NEW DIRECTIONS

While Gates was participating in the active campus life of Yale, as well as growing more politically and culturally aware, he was still considering more traditional options for the future, such as studying to become a lawyer. He had decided against studying literature and, instead, to major in political science. What drew his attention more than the study of political theory and practice was the history of American politics. He also took classes in general history and African American studies. Finally, Gates also enrolled in the "Five Year B.A." program in which students were allowed to take a year's leave from their studies to pursue a related nonacademic interest. For Gates, the interest was simple: to travel to Africa, the continent that had so fascinated him ever since he was a young boy studying the handout maps in elementary school and reading about the different African nations.

TANZANIA

In 1970, Gates made his way to Tanzania, a sub-Saharan country in East Africa, where he was slated to work in the hospital at an Anglican mission. Tanzania is the largest nation in East Africa, which also includes Kenya and Uganda. The country is known for its spectacular landscape, consisting of three main regions: the islands and the coastal plains to the east; the inland plateau; and the highlands. Among the most notable geographic landmarks is the Great Rift Valley that runs through central Tanzania. The valley offers breathtaking vicws that include several lakes, such as Lake Rukwa, Lake Tanganyika, and Lake Evasi. Mount Kilimanjaro is also found in Tanzania.

The country is among the oldest continuously inhabited areas in the world; in Tanzania, archeologists have uncovered both human and animal remains dating back more than two million years. Scientists believe that the region was first inhabited by groups of hunter-gathers such as the cushitic and Khoisan peoples. Approximately 2,000 years ago, Bantu-speaking peoples began to arrive from western Africa, followed by a group known as the Nilotic pastoralists. As early as the first century AD, trade was established between Arabia and the East African coast. Primarily, the Arabs established these early coastal trading centers, and it appears that relations between the Arab traders and sub-Saharan Africans were cordial. During this period, too, Arab traders began exploring further into the interior of Tanzania in search of slaves and ivory.[1]

The first white visitors to the country were the Portuguese, who arrived in the late fifteenth century. Unlike the Arabs, whose influence was extensive, the Portuguese established at best, a tenuous control in the country. Beginning in 1776, the French came to Tanzania, drawn in part by the burgeoning slave trade. By the nineteenth century, European missionaries showed a strong interest in Tanzania, along with explorers intent on mapping the geography of the county. These primarily geographic expeditions were followed by the activities of the celebrated doctor David Livingstone, who, in 1866, set out to expose the horrors of the slave trade and, by opening up legitimate trade with the interior, sought to destroy the slave trade at its roots.

Livingstone's journey led to the later expeditions of H. M. Stanley and V. L. Cameron. Spurred on by Livingstone's work and example, a number of missionary societies began to take an interest in East Africa after 1860. By the late nineteenth century, Germany, which had been expanding its colonial empire into Africa, conquered the regions that are now Tanzania, Rwanda, and Burundi and incorporated them into German East Africa. With Germany's defeat in the First World War, however, the region fell under British rule until 1961, when Tanzania declared its independence.[2]

A SON OF AFRICA, BUT NOT AN AFRICAN

Upon his arrival in Tanzania, Gates headed for the small village of Kilimatinde, where the Anglican mission to which he had been assigned was located. The village had fewer than 500 inhabitants. The Kilimatinde hospital was approximately an 80-bed facility run by the Anglican Church on the edge of the Rift Valley; it served not only the village but also the large area surrounding Kilimatinde. Power for the hospital came from a large generator; water was pumped in from an underground source and had to be boiled to eliminate contaminants. There was a small theater for performing surgery as well as a small pharmacy. Although he had no formal medical training, Gates's job was to administer anesthesia during operations. While in Tanzania, Gates lived among the Wagogo villagers and the Masai herdsmen. Like many young African Americans during he 1960s and 1970s, Gates entertained a romantic vision of Africa. Once he arrived in Tanzania, it was quickly dashed. At one point he wrote:

> My very first night was spent in tears, wondering what could have possessed me to pledge to live in a village of 500 people with no electricity, telephones, televisions, or running water, and where the "express bus" (which delivered both telegrams and the mail) passed through just twice a week.[3]

Gates soon realized that he had no idea of what he had gotten himself into. He later stated in an interview, "I was a tabula rasa and on me was being inscribed: Mother Africa from the Ground Up. I probably would have said that you were a racist if you thought that Africans still lived in mud huts. So I get there and everybody lives in mud huts. It's worse than I imagined."[4]

After six months of living and working in Kilimantinde, Gates decided to travel throughout Africa. During the course of his travels,

Gates met another young American, Lawrence Biddle Weeks, at a dock in Dar es Salaam, the capital city of Tanzania. Weeks had recently graduated from Harvard. During the course of their conversation, Weeks stated that he had always wanted to go from the Cape in South African to Cairo, Egypt. Gates was on a personal quest of his own, hoping to cross the Equator. As Gates later stated, "We flipped a coin and the Equator won. We went from the Indian Ocean to the Atlantic Ocean without ever leaving the ground."[5]

The journey across Africa was an exhilarating time for Gates. He and Weeks hitchhiked from Dar es Salaam and then traveled north to Kenya, where they visited the cities of Mombassa and Nairobi. They continued to Kampala, Uganda, arriving a day after Idi Amin's 1971 coup. They were stopped at the Congolese border and denied entry: they did not realize that they were expected to offer "dash," a small bribe, in order to enter the country. They went to Kigali, the capital of Rwanda, where they managed to secure new visas. Then it was on to Goma, which is situated on Lake Kivu. They rode on the back of a truck full of empty beer bottles as they made their way through tropical rain forests and the African bush country before arriving at Kisangani, an important port located on the Congo River. From there, Gates and his companion caught a riverboat for the five-day journey to their final destination: Kinshasa in the Democratic Republic of the Congo. The trip took more than two months to complete, and while Gates found it to be one of the most exhilarating experiences of his life it was, at the same time, almost the deadliest. During the journey, he became seriously ill with dysentery and lost almost 30 pounds.

The trip to Africa was one of many that Gates had the opportunity to take during the next two decades. But it was on his first trip that he realized sporting an Afro and wearing a dashiki, a brightly colored shirt made from African fabrics and prints, did not bring him any closer to being African. As he wrote later, he was "an African son but not of Africa." He also realized that the Wagogo villagers and farmers as well as the Masai herdsmen were not "simple extensions of my putative African family but peoples with their own discrete histories and their own unique cultures." Still, during the course of his travels, he awakened to the close cultural and historical ties that Africans and African Americans shared.[6]

A CHANGE OF COURSE

Upon his return from Africa, Gates knew he would need to find some kind of interim employment before he returned to Yale in the fall. While in Africa, he had written to John David Rockefeller IV, who was serving as the Secretary of State for West Virginia. Rockefeller had decided to run for governor. Gates wrote to Rockefeller asking for a job working in his campaign. To his surprise and delight, when he returned to Piedmont, a letter from Rockefeller offering Gates a job was waiting for him. Gates moved to Charleston, where he helped with Rockefeller's campaign. Even though Rockefeller lost the election, Gates still considered his time well spent.

It was while working for Rockefeller's campaign that Gates met his future wife Sharon Adams. Adams, also from West Virginia, was a 22-year-old white woman who had recently quit her job as a freight dispatcher in Charleston to work for the Rockefeller campaign. Soon after she met Gates, the two became involved romantically. For Adams, this was the first time she had ever been involved with a black man. She recalled later her first impression of Gates: "I'd never been anywhere, and here was this young man who'd trekked across Africa . . . There was a lightheartedness about him. He was absolutely brilliant. I just found him completely irresistible."[7]

In 1972, with the campaign ended, Adams moved to New Haven with Gates, where she took a job as a real estate rental agent while Gates attended classes. But although the couple's landlord found their relationship exotic, their neighbors did not. The couple also had to contend with Sharon's parents, who had made it very clear to their daughter they would not approve of her dating black men. Adams recalled in an interview "when I was 14 or 15, my mother said to me, 'The only thing that will ever make me stop loving you is if you get addicted to drugs or if you date a black guy.'" Adams did not tell her parents she was dating a black man, but before she moved to New Haven, her mother met the couple at a restaurant. The meeting did not go well, and Adams's mother made her daughter promise not to tell her father about Gates.[8]

Even with his studies, Gates felt at loose ends. Not long after his return, one of his friends, who was the editor of the school newspaper, the Yale *Daily News*, asked Gates if he would be interested in writing about his experiences in Africa. Gates agreed; the article turned into a series of columns that got the attention of students and faculty alike. In fact, one of his columns earned him the praise of one of the campus's most respected scholars, the historian John Morton Blum. As Gates recalled in a 2003 interview:

> One day John Blum called me out from the podium of this huge class, Politics and Culture in Twentieth Century America. This was a class that everyone took. It was packed. He said, "Is Mr. Gates in the room?" I said yes. I stood up and he said, "I really enjoyed your essay in today's student newspaper." Everyone looked at me like, who's that guy? I went like, wow, man, you know? But I had to sit down all cool, and go like, "Oh, yeah, it happens to me every day." Inside I was hooked. I went to him and said, "Would you be my adviser?"[9]

The association with Blum proved advantageous to Gates in many ways. Realizing that he needed to declare a major, Gates now decided on history. He had already taken six history courses and needed only 12 to complete the major. Blum agreed to take him on as an advisee and to serve as Gates's mentor.[10]

In addition to Blum, William McFeeley, another historian, also served as a source of inspiration for Gates. McFeeley taught the African American history courses at Yale. Gates remembers that there were several hundred students taking one of McFeeley's classes. At the end of every lecture, one of the more militant African American students stood up, and declared: "Yeah, yeah, I'll ask it nice, but when are we going to get a black person in here?" Professor McFeeley, who was white, took no offense and replied, "We need to get more people of color into universities such as Yale, but in the meantime, I'm doing the best that I can." McFeeley's patience in the face of critical and even hostile questions made a tremendous impression on Gates. It was a lesson that he never forgot, reflecting on it often when, years later, he began his own teaching career.[11]

During his senior year, Gates applied to become a Yale Scholar of the House, a prestigious honor in which 12 students are chosen to work on projects of their own instead of attending classes. The idea for the program originated during the war years, between 1940 and 1945, with the first students, mostly veterans from World War II, accepted in 1946. The program proved immensely successful and has continued ever since. Gates decided to spend his time writing a book about his experiences working on the Jay Rockefeller gubernatorial campaign, which he titled *The Once and Future King.*[12]

Gates's work so impressed his advisor, John Blum, that Blum told Gates he had the makings of a successful journalist or an academic. Clearly, Gates had demonstrated that he was a good writer. Perhaps instead of pursuing a career in law, he should think about other avenues in which his talents would be put to better use. Gates already realized that he enjoyed doing archival research as well as writing. He spent hours at the university libraries, particularly the Beinecke Rare Book Library, where he immersed himself in the James Weldon Johnson Collection, which contained materials pertaining to African American history. With the encouragement of his professors, Gates began thinking about how he might contribute to the field of African American studies.

CAMBRIDGE

In 1973, Gates graduated from Yale, summa cum laude, with a B.A. in history. He also had been accepted for a Mellon Fellowship to continue his studies at Clare College, which was part of Cambridge University in England. For Gates, going to Cambridge was another goal. As a young boy, while his friends talked of becoming famous athletes, Gates dreamed of becoming a Rhodes Scholar, a prestigious international scholarship that allows students to study at Oxford University. Although not a Rhodes, the Mellon Scholarship was just as impressive, and for Gates, perhaps even more so since he was the first African American ever to be awarded the honor. In a later interview, Gates recalled what happened after he received the news:

> I rushed back to Calvin College at Yale and I called home to Piedmont. My dad answered the phone. I said, "Daddy, Daddy, put Mom on the phone." She got on the extension and he said,

> "What, boy? What's wrong?" I said, "I got a Mellon Fellowship. I got a Mellon Fellowship. I'm the first black American to get a Mellon Fellowship." And my father said, "A Mellon Fellowship? You're the first black American?" He said, "Huh, they're going to call it the Watermelon Fellowship from now on."[13]

As if things could not get any better, Gates also had been offered a job with *Time* magazine as a writer. The day after his graduation, Gates boarded the *Queen Elizabeth II* and was on his way to Southampton and from thence to Cambridge. For the remainder of the summer, Gates wrote for *Time* magazine until it was time to begin classes in the fall.[14]

Gates fell in love with Cambridge. As he recalled in an interview, "I learned to speak in paragraphs, and became a citizen of the world; I went to the theatre and became addicted to Indian food," though Gates found the English food wanting. Gates also enjoyed going to London, which became one of his favorite cities in the world. Those visits were also a revelation for him; he was fascinated when he heard black English people talk like their white counterparts, since "in America, black people tend to sound like each other."[15]

At Cambridge Gates rediscovered his true passion: literature. As much as he enjoyed studying history, it was the study of texts that engaged him the most. Unfortunately, when Gates arrived at Clare College, his instructors were not as welcoming or as encouraging as he had found at Yale. Stuart Hall, professor emeritus of sociology at the Open University, says Gates "romanticized Britain and got things wrong; there was not a lot of depth but there was enthusiasm." His professors also informed Gates that there was no place at Cambridge for the study of African American literature. They believed that the writings of blacks lacked the rigor to be included in the curriculum. In an interview, Gates described the atmosphere that he had encountered at Cambridge:

> I was told in no uncertain terms that I could write about Milton or Shakespeare, maybe even Pound and Eliot, who had just recently been introduced to the canon, but certainly not anything

> African or African-American. And after months of arguing, they allowed me to choose as a topic the Enlightenment, the 18th century, and to look at how Europeans wrote about the first African—and what we would now call African-American writers who were published in English and French and German and Dutch. So it was sort of a compromise.[16]

TWO IMPORTANT FRIENDS

Discouraged by his studies and homesick for America, Gates began looking for some kind of familiarity. Although Sharon had joined him, he was still lonely for company. Many people he spoke to asked him if he had yet met a young man named Anthony Appiah, who Gates figured was another black man. Soon the two were introduced and would become very close friends.

Kwame Anthony Appiah was as different from Gates as he could be. Then just 18 years old, he was the son of a very prominent lawyer and politician from Ghana; he was also the nephew of the King of the Asante, Otumfuo Nana Opoku Ware II. On his mother's side, he was the grandson of Sir Stafford Cripps, former chancellor of the British Labour Party. Gates was very taken with his new friend, calling him "the smartest human being I have ever met." Gates also tried to emulate Appiah by wearing small silk neck scarves and growing his hair like Appiah's. Like his role models at Yale, Glenn DeChabert and Armstead Robinson, Gates was inspired by Appiah's intelligence and outlook on life. Soon the young man was a steady visitor to Gates's and Sharon's home.[17]

Gates, in turn, fascinated Appiah. In a later interview, Appiah described their early friendship:

> Skip was sort of an evangelist for African American causes about which I knew nothing. He seemed worldly to me. He had a big Afro, and a big white felt hat, the kind you saw in blaxploitation movies. And as a stringer for *Time*, he was going to Paris to see James Baldwin and Josephine Baker, and Kathleen and Eldridge Cleaver. After I met Skip, I began to learn to think about race in western culture.[18]

Through Appiah, Gates met Wole Soyinka, a Nigerian writer who had been imprisoned for more than two years. Known later in the West as the "Shakespeare of Africa," Soyinka wrote a memoir called *The Man Died* while imprisoned. Following his release, he fled to England because of death threats from the Nigerian government. He had come to Cambridge to teach.

Before meeting Soyinka, Gates, hoping to impress him, read up on African philosophy and literature. In particular, he studied a book by the author Janheinz Jahn called *Muntu*, in which the author tried to "reduce 2,000 African cultures to five recurring principles." As Gates later related, "This was supposedly the thing that gave Africans culture and unity." Gates would later learn that the book and its thesis were totally wrong. But at the time, the book was very popular, so Gates, hoping to impress Soyinka, memorized the five principles.[19]

When the two finally met, they began talking. "Finally," Gates recalled, "he looks at me, and he kind of looks at my Afro, and says, 'Well it's obvious you don't know too much about African literature.'" Soyinka also said it was good that Gates did not try to talk to him about the *Muntu* nonsense. Gates replied, "Muntu? Never heard of it."[20]

Soyinka had come to Cambridge intending to teach, but because the members of the English Department at Cambridge did not believe that an African literature existed, they denied Soyinka a permanent position. Instead, he taught a class called "Myth, Literature and the African World." Gates was his only student. At one point, Gates went to visit Soyinka at his office. When he arrived, he found a note on the door: "Unavailable. Come back in a week." It turned out that Soyinka was busy writing the play *Death and the King's Horseman*, for which he later won the Nobel Prize in 1986. Soyinka convinced Gates to study literature, specifically African American literature, and to trace its lineage in the literary traditions of Africa and the Caribbean. For Gates, Soyinka's teaching marked the beginning of his love affair with African and African American literature. Soyinka remembered Gates as being "passionate about recovering the African portion of his origins."[21]

His two new African friends exercised a profound influence on Gates. He credits his interest in, and his passion for, African studies to the teaching of Soyinka and to his friendship with Appiah. Indeed,

Gates believes that if not for these two men, he would have never chosen to study African or African American literature.[22]

DISCOVERING THEORY

In addition to his love of literature, Gates also discovered the study of literary theory, or the study of the nature of literature and of the methods of analyzing it. Gates knew little about theory, as he wrote later:

> I didn't even know what literary theory was. When I wrote my first essay, my supervisor said it was the worst essay she had ever read, because I didn't know how to explicate a text. I went to her and I said, "Surely there must be books to teach me this method?" She said, "No, no, you're born with it. It's some sort of sensibility that you get through your genes." Well, being a practical American, I went to the bookstore and I asked for the literary criticism section and I bought it—the whole section. I bought one discrete title of each book, and I went back and I read those books and I ended up doing very well, thank goodness.[23]

OTHER PROBLEMS

During his two years at Cambridge, Gates maintained friendly relations with Sharon Adams's family over the phone, though her father still had no idea that Gates was black. She admitted later, "It never occurred to Dad that Skip might be black." The deception was hard on the couple, but her mother had made it clear that her father was not to know about Gates's skin color. The charade continued until the couple returned to the United States. Even though Gates believes that Sharon's mother made the right decision, as her father was an avowed racist, Sharon decided to go ahead and tell her father the truth. As her mother predicted, her father did not take the news well.[24]

Eventually, Sharon's father was "shamed" into accepting Gates. But Gates, though he could forgive, admitted that it was harder to forget. As he later admitted, "you don't get over something like that. It never did not happen . . . My mother never got over it."[25]

THE RAINBOW COALITION

By 1974, Gates had completed his MA at Cambridge. He thought of giving law school a try, applied, was accepted, but then decided that being a lawyer was not what he wanted to do. He returned to New Haven to begin work on a doctoral dissertation. When he decided to drop out of law school, he went to see a family friend, Charles Davis, who also happened to be head of the Afro-American studies department at Yale. Davis told Gates, "Look. I'm so glad you're dropping out of law school. I'll give you a job." When Davis asked Gates what he could do, what skills he had, Gates replied that he could type. It was thus that Gates came to be secretary to the Afro-American studies department at Yale, a position he held from October 1, 1975, to June 30, 1976. Afterward, he was promoted to a lecturer convertible, which meant that once Gates received his PhD, he would become an assistant professor. Davis joked that Gates's promotion was the biggest any secretary ever got in the history of Yale. More than that, because of Davis, Gates was now back on track. He was grateful for Davis's intercession because, as he later said, "Charles had vision. He told me I should be an academic, that I should stick with it, that one day I would be chair of Afro-American studies at Yale."[26]

It was while at work on his dissertation that Gates got to know a number of noted scholars who helped him. Among them were two African American professors. The first was the aforementioned Charles Davis, the first black master of John C. Calhoun College at Yale, and the first African American tenured in the English department. It was Davis who supervised Gates's dissertation.

The second was African American historian John W. Blassingame, who was a well-known scholar and historian of slavery in the United States. Blassingame, who was a member of the Yale faculty for almost 30 years, devoted himself to the preservation of primary source materials that told the story of the African American experience, especially slavery. Among his best known works were *Slave Testimony: Two Centuries of Letters, Speeches, Interviews, and Autobiographies*, published in 1977, which was a collection of autobiographical materials about and by former slaves. Blassingame also edited the six volumes of the *Papers of Frederick Douglass*, the noted African American abolitionist.

Gates viewed Blassingame as "the king of archivists." Blassingame taught Gates the importance of history and historical documents that recorded people, places, and things at a certain time in history. For Blassingame, the historian's job was to recover those realities so they could be studied, so they might answer questions and then be preserved for others. Persistence was key to Blassingame; in order to find the historical truth, a historian must be willing to go the distance to uncover those documents pertinent to telling the historical story.

Blassingame and Gates also became friends. The two often met with other African American scholars at a little restaurant in New Haven, the Naples Pizza Shop, to have breakfast and discuss matters of common interest and concern. Gates soon came to cherish these meetings, eagerly sharing with the others his archival discoveries. His companions then offered suggestions and advice for Gates as he continued his research and writing. Gates also worked with such literary scholars as Raymond Williams, George Steiner, and John Holloway. Along the way, Gates came to an important realization: if he could combine his love for archival work with literary theory and apply both to the study of African American literature, he might make important contributions and help to validate a field that he feared was perilously close to disappearing from the curriculum of many colleges and universities in the United States.[27]

NOTES

1. United Republic of Tanzania, http://www.tanzania.go.tz/historyf.html.

2. Medicine Uncharted, Org. "Kilimatinde Hospital," http://www.medicineuncharted.org/destinations/Tanzania_Kilimatinde.html.

3. Henry Louis Gates, *Wonders of the African World* (New York: Borzoi Books, 1999), 13.

4. Cheryl Bentsen, "Head Negro in Charge," *Boston Magazine*, July 23, 2009, http://www.bostonmagazine.com/articles/Henry_Louis_Gates_Jr/page5.

5. Bruce Cole, "Interview: Henry Louis Gates," 2002, http://www.neh.gov/whoweare/gates/interview.html.

6. Gates, *Wonders of the African World*, 13.

7. Cheryl Bentsen, "Head Negro in Charge," *Boston Magazine*, July 23, 2009, http://www.bostonmagazine.com/articles/Henry_Louis_Gates_Jr/page5.

8. Ibid.

9. Cole, "Interview: Henry Louis Gates."

10. Ibid.

11. Ibid.

12. Walter L. Goldfrank, "The Scholars of the House Program at Yale: Praise from the Faculty, Student Criticism," *The Harvard Crimson*, November 22, 1958, http://www.thecrimson.com/article/1958/11/22/the-scholars-of-the-house-program/; Bruce Cole, "Interview: Henry Louis Gates," 2002, http://www.neh.gov/whoweare/gates/interview.html.

13. Cole, "Interview: Henry Louis Gates."

14. Ibid.

15. Maya Jaggi, "Review: Profile: Henry the first: Henry Louis Gates: Born into a poor family in West Virginia, he went on to study at Yale and became one of the US's leading African American academics. At Harvard, he has built a flagship department but a public row about race and politics now threatens its future," *The Guardian* (London), July 6, 2002, 20.

16. "Booknotes: Colored People by Henry Louis Gates, Jr.," October 9, 1994, http://www.booknotes.org/Watch/60633-1/Henry+Louis+Gates.aspx

17. Bentsen, "Head Negro in Charge," 4.

18. Ibid.

19. Ibid., 5.

20. Ibid., 4.

21. Cole, "Interview: Henry Louis Gates"; Cheryl Bentsen, "Head Negro in Charge," *Boston Magazine*, July 23, 2009, http://www.bostonmagazine.com/articles/Henry_Louis_Gates_Jr/page5.

22. "Booknotes: Colored People by Henry Louis Gates, Jr.," October 9, 1994, http://www.booknotes.org/Watch/60633-1/Henry+Louis+Gates.aspx

23. Cole, “Interview: Henry Louis Gates.”

24. Bentsen, “Head Negro in Charge,” 4.

25. Ibid.

26. Cole, “Interview: Henry Louis Gates”; Bentsen, “Head Negro in Charge,” 5.

27. Cole, “Interview: Henry Louis Gates.”

Chapter 6

TAKING BACK THE PAST

To understand better why Gates's work had such an impact on American literary thought in general and on the study of African American literature in particular, it is important to understand the legacy of African American literature in American literary history. Surprising as it may seem today, African American literature was not a field that drew a lot of serious scholarship. Although several African American scholars undertook important studies of African American writing, it was not until Henry Louis Gates's work appeared that a distinct and unique literary theory using strictly African and African American references was considered viable.

In part, this has been due to the relatively limited scope afforded black writers in terms of subject matter. This limitation made it difficult for subsequent generations of black writers who, having little to guide them from their own perspective, often turned to the works of white writers for inspiration instead of looking to black writers who preceded them. The noted African American writer and intellectual Lindsay Patterson stated the problem bluntly: "the black writer has been cheated out of a wellspring; but more than that, he has been made to feel that his ancestors contributed only a 'shuffling' stereotype to the literary developments in this country."[1]

THE AFRICAN AMERICAN LITERARY TRADITION

The history of the African American literary tradition is as old and diverse as the American nation. In almost all writings of American blacks, three themes occur: the battle against a racist white society, the search for an African American identity, and maintaining and recording the unique and rich cultural traditions of black life. The end result is a literature that tells the history, the heartbreak, and the heroism—in short, the rich experience of African Americans.

African American literature dates to the slaves' arrival in the British North American colonies in 1619, when the slaves, in an attempt to preserve their own cultural traditions, created first an oral tradition and, subsequently, a literature of their own. It is a literature that was forged from the harsh reality of their lives. Almost from the moment they set foot on North American soil, Africans lived with the continual threat to erase their sense of identity. Except in rare circumstances, literacy among African Americans, particularly among slaves, was discouraged; at worst, it was forbidden by law under pain of punishment and even death. This denial of the chance to read and write only increased the determination of many African Americans to learn; to read and write represented a kind of freedom and power to them. If African Americans were to succeed within the constraints of white society, it was imperative that they become literate. The struggle to maintain their African roots became, over time, a kind of cultural synthesis that combined both African and Western European influences. The earliest writings of African Americans focused on freedom and were largely influenced by religious tracts and the Bible, which began to move them away from established African literary traditions.

The first African American to be published in America was a young woman by the name of Phillis Wheatley. Her life was highly unusual; enslaved at a young age and taken to Boston, she was educated by her white masters. She showed a gift for writing poetry and was encouraged by her white owners and their daughter. Wheatley's first poem, "On Messrs. Hussey and Coffin," was published when she was just

12 years old, in 1767. Wheatley also had a patron in the Countess of Huntingdon, Selina Hastings, who financed the publication of her first book of poetry, *Poems*, published in 1769. Wheatley was especially fond of the elegiac poetry style, which mirrored the type of oration taught to her as a child in Africa. Her elegy on the popular evangelical Methodist minister George Whitefield, who died in 1771, brought her great success in the colonies. Her popularity in both the United States and England eventually freed her from her bonds of slavery in 1773. That same year, 39 of her poems were published in London as *Poems on Various Subjects, Religious and Moral* and marked the first book to be published by an African American.

There also appeared another type of writing that focused on the injustices blacks endured in America; many of these writings began calling for the end of slavery and racial discrimination. An early example was the letter written in 1791 by the gifted astronomer Benjamin Banneker to Thomas Jefferson, then secretary of state and later president of the United States. Banneker appealed to Jefferson to recognize blacks as the equals of whites.[2]

By the beginning of the nineteenth century, African American writing turned away from its previous emphasis on religion and began to focus more on political and social issues, particularly slavery. Even though the United States had abolished the importation of slaves in 1808, slavery continued to flourish, particularly in the South. A North Carolina slave, George Moses Horton, became the first African American writer to protest the practice of slavery in 1829 with the publication of his book, *The Hope of Liberty*. That same year, David Walker published the *Appeal, in Four Articles*, in which he attacked the arguments in favor of slavery and racism and urged blacks to use violence if necessary to end their bondage. Walker's writing is thought to have influenced Virginia slave rebel Nat Turner, who led a bloody slave insurrection in Southampton County, Virginia, in 1831, in which some 60 whites were killed.

With the creation of the abolitionist movement in the North, African American writers found an even larger audience. The antislavery newspaper *The Liberator*, established in 1831 by William Lloyd Garrison, helped to popularize a specific genre of African American literature: the slave narrative. Titles such as *A Narrative of the*

Adventures and Escape of Moses Roper, published in 1837, and the international best seller *Narrative of the Life of Frederick Douglass, an American Slave*, published in 1845, brought acclaim and success for some former slaves. One New England observer, Ephraim Peabody, saw the narratives as "new department" in literature, while another writer, Theodore Parker, suggested that the slave narratives were the only true American form of writing. But the practitioners of this new genre also intended to denounce slavery, to encourage others to oppose it, and, if possible, to bring it to an end.

Another slave autobiography initially overlooked during this period but later hailed as an important work was Harriet Jacobs's *Incidents in the Life of a Slave Girl*, published in 1861. The book focused on the life of a slave woman, with a particular emphasis on her relationships with her master, the white man who became the father of her children, and her children themselves. It was a harbinger of the themes and concerns that characterized much of the later writing by African American women.[3] To resist the sexual advances of her master and to protect herself from his wrath, Jacobs, whose real name was Linda Brent, took a white lover who fathered two children with her. To escape the rigors and injustice of slavery, Jacobs subsequently abandoned her children and fled north, hoping one day to rescue them from bondage. The essence of her argument in *Incidents in the Life of a Slave Girl* was that slavery was wrong and immoral not only because it exposed blacks to cruelty and injustice, but also because it also prevented them from living upright and virtuous lives. As long as she was enslaved, Jacobs could not be a faithful wife or a dutiful mother to her children. On the contrary, slavery had forced her into an illicit relationship with a white man whom she did not love and, in any event, could not marry, and compelled her to forsake her children. Freedom had to come first, before she could aspire to virtue or duty.

While the slave narratives had familiarized whites with a world largely unknown to them, African American fiction also explored many of the same ideas and themes. The publication of a previously unknown manuscript, which Gates discovered in 2002, *The Bondwoman's Narrative, by Hannah Crafts, a Fugitive Slave*, opened up the landscape of African American literature. John Brown Russwurm, who published as a poet, fugitive slave narrator, essayist, travel writer, dramatist, historian, and novelist, published the first novel by an African American in 1853 with *Clotel; or, The President's Daughter.* The plot was based on the rumored affair between Thomas Jefferson and a slave named Sally Hemings.

During the second half of the nineteenth century, social reformer Frances Ellen Watkins Harper emerged as one of the more prolific and popular African American writers. Harper's poetry, though technically dependent on the popular white male poets of the period such as Henry Wadsworth Longfellow and John Greenleaf Whittier, carried strong antislavery sentiments. Her first book, *Poems on Miscellaneous Subjects*, published in 1854, went through almost two dozen editions during the course of two decades. Among her other works are the first short story by an African American, "The Two Offers," published in 1859; the biblical narrative *Moses, a Story of the Nile*, published in 1869; and a novel about an octoroon heroine, *Iola Leroy, or Shadows Uplifted*, that was published in 1892.[4]

Very little African American writing focused on the Civil War; in fact, the war went largely unnoticed in African American literature of any type. What many literary scholars consider one of the most powerful pieces of writing to emerge from the period is the *Journal of Charlotte Forten (1854–1892)*, kept by Charlotte Forten Grimké, an African American woman who was the granddaughter of a wealthy African American sail maker and abolitionist. Grimké later went on to teach in the Sea Islands off the coast of South Carolina during the war. Elizabeth Keckley's autobiography, *Behind the Scenes; or Thirty Years a Slave, and Four Years in the White House*, published in 1868, recounts her life as a slave and later as seamstress to Mary Todd Lincoln.

After the war, African American literature almost came to a standstill. For many African Americans, the promise of Reconstruction was tinged with despair and a growing awareness that, despite emancipation, things really had not changed much for them. If anything, times were worse as blacks were experiencing a deepening racial animosity, particularly in the South. With their civil rights stripped away and Jim Crow laws that imposed racial discrimination as a matter of course, African Americans found themselves relegated to a tightly segregated world.

The rise of legal segregation and of vigilante oppression after Reconstruction diminished but did not destroy African American literature. With the rise of black newspapers and journals such as *The Voice of the Negro* and *The Colored American*, African American literature was revived and revitalized. In 1884, the poet Albery A. Whitman published, "Rape of Florida." In 1899, Sutton Griggs published *Imperium in Imperio*, the first of five privately printed novels that showcased Griggs's ideas about Black Nationalism and the future of African Americans in the United States.[5]

The major new talents of the age, however, were the fiction writer Charles W. Chesnutt and the poet and novelist Paul Laurence Dunbar. A talented poet, essayist, and short story writer, Chesnutt managed to keep his racial identity a secret from his readers, even as his work was published in major publications such as the *Atlantic Monthly*. Yet Chesnutt drew heavily on the black folklore of the antebellum South, while at the same time offering readers a picture of the harsh realities of slave life. He also boldly explored the racial tensions of his day.

Dunbar was the first African American to achieve national fame as a poet with his 1896 book *Lyrics of Lowly Life*, followed in 1899 by *Lyrics from the Hearthside*. Dunbar drew his inspiration from stereotypes of black life drawn from the minstrel tradition and incorporated black dialect into his verse. For these reasons, his poems were immensely popular among whites, but perhaps not as much among African Americans. Eventually, Dunbar came to regret having gained literary recognition by perpetuating black stereotypes and using black dialect. He lamented that even as he composed poems in standard English, he would more likely be remembered as the poet of a "A jingle in a broken tongue."[6]

W. E. B. DU BOIS AND *THE SOULS OF BLACK FOLK*

An event still widely considered the watershed moment in African American literature came in 1903 with the publication of W. E. B. Du Bois's epochal *The Souls of Black Folk*. The book, which consisted primarily of essays on black history and culture, transformed African American literature and thought. Appearing two years after the publication of noted African American educator and leader Booker T. Washington's autobiography, *Up from Slavery*, Du Bois's book illustrated a far more complex and conflicted story of African American life, culture, and identity. Du Bois went on to write a number of other books, historical, sociological, biographical, and fictional, as well as to serve as editor of the magazine *The Crisis*, the official journal of the newly formed National Association for the Advancement of Colored People (NAACP). Du Bois had a tremendous impact on future black writers, who often cited his work and example as among their chief influences.[7]

One of the most dominant themes in Du Bois's writing is the belief that art should not be created for art's sake; in the case of African Americans, art had to serve a political and social purpose. Good art, whether it is a novel, poem, or painting, must lift up the race, an argument that continues to resonate among African American writers today. One writer who took this belief to heart was James Weldon Johnson, who, in 1912, published *The Autobiography of an Ex-Coloured Man*, often described as the first noteworthy psychological novel in African American fiction. The Jamaican-born Claude McKay also subscribed to Du Bois's belief. His poetry used conventional lyrics to call for greater assertiveness on the part of African Americans. His best-known poem, "If We Must Die," was widely read by blacks as a brave call to strike back at white injustice and brutality.[8]

THE HARLEM RENAISSANCE

African American writers in the first decades of the twentieth century created the figure that Alain Locke called "the New Negro" and ushered in an artistic movement that came to be known as the Harlem Renaissance. The center of the movement was Harlem in New York City. Arriving from the South or the West Indies, many African Americans settled in Harlem, which had originally been home to middle- and upper-middle-class whites. Harlem soon became the center of African American culture, a place where black writers, artists, and musicians could congregate and where whites could go hear the sounds of jazz and the blues. By the 1920s, Harlem was "the Negro capital of the world."[9]

Along with an increased interest in African American music, dance, and art was a growing awareness of and admiration for African American literature. Writers such as Langston Hughes and Zora Neale Hurston, who often worked in the idiom of the common people, nevertheless elevated African American folk literature into a high art. Hughes drew on traditional verse, melding it to jazz and blues rhythms. Putting the African American dialect to different uses than Paul Laurence Dunbar had, Hughes at the same time created a new form of free verse. Meanwhile, Hurston, whose 1935 anthropological study *Mules and Men* recounted African American folk culture, became one of the most celebrated writers associated with the Harlem Renaissance. Both she and Hughes helped to solidify and elevate African American writing, not only celebrating African American creativity and culture but also providing a mirror in which African Americans could see an authentic self.[10]

PROTEST LITERATURE

By the 1940s, the Harlem Renaissance was dead; the stock market crash of 1929 and the ensuing Great Depression ended the vibrant and pulsating rhythms that had driven life in Harlem during the 1920s, "when," as the historian David Levering Lewis has written, "Harlem was in vogue." Although African American writers were still a part of the literary scene in the United States, it was not until the 1940s that the next significant development in African American literature emerged. The social realism of the 1940s, also known as protest literature, focused on the current problems of African American society instead of looking to the past. This literary protest movement has been compared to the muckraking journalism of an earlier era in its effort to expose the social evils of racism, discrimination, and poverty in rough, hard-hitting, and often ungainly prose.[11]

By this time, large numbers of African Americans had migrated to the North in search of jobs and a better life. This Great Migration, which had begun at the turn of the century and swelled during the years of the First World War, by the early 1940s saw thousands of blacks streaming into such large northern cities h as New York, Chicago, Detroit, St. Louis, and Kansas City. In many cases, what awaited them were low-paying jobs and homes in overcrowded and unsanitary ghettoes.

Native Son, which Richard Wright published in 1940, depicted the gradual degradation of the African American in this new urban world and opened the door for this next wave of African American literature. Wright had little interest in carrying on Du Bois's injunction to elevate the race. Along with Ann Petry, author of the 1946 novel *The Street*, Wright was more interested in showing how the harsh urban world could gradually destroy an individual's character, and how ill equipped blacks were by education and experience to cope with such a hostile environment.[12]

The decade of the 1950s brought forth a wellspring of African American writers who not only transcended the genres of fiction and poetry but opened new doors as well. Considered one of the seminal novels of American literature was Ralph Ellison's 1952 work, *Invisible Man*, which relates the alienation and disillusionment that African Americans felt. But for many Americans, white and black, Ellison's novel rose above racial distinctions to become a universal story of the dark side of the American experience.[13]

Certainly one of the most significant African American writers of the late twentieth century was James Baldwin. A gifted novelist, Baldwin was also an accomplished essayist and literary critic. His words were filled with a passion and power not seen since W. E. B. Du Bois. It was Baldwin's words that helped explain how African Americans felt during the explosive years of the civil rights movement. Although he spent many years abroad, Baldwin believed that living in a culture unlike one's own made it necessary to reflect a person's own culture and civilization. For Henry Louis Gates, Jr., it was reading James Baldwin that made him realize for the first time the literary power and history of black writing.

THE BLACK ARTS MOVEMENT

The period of the 1960s gave rise to the Black Arts movement, also known as the Black Aesthetics movement; it was also was the first major African American artistic and literary movement since the Harlem Renaissance of the 1920s. With the coming of the Black

Power movement and the continuing struggle for civil rights raged, black writers of the Black Arts movement set out to define what it meant to be a black writer in a white culture. Unlike the writers of the Harlem Renaissance who explored the inner identity of the African American, the writers of the Black Arts movement wrote about defining themselves before being scrutinized and defined by white society. They also saw themselves as rebelling against white America as well as the middle class and were strong supporters of the Black Nationalist ideology. Leading writers in this movement included Amiri Baraka (LeRoi Jones), who wrote powerful poetry and plays, and Haki R. Madhubuti (Don L. Lee), who was known for his explosive poetry and essays.

The Black Arts movement wanted to write novels, poems, and plays that would be meaningful to all African Americans. All different types of black cultural expression, from the jazz music of John Coltrane to the soul music of popular singer James Brown, inspired them. They also drew inspiration from the everyday street talk and slang heard in black neighborhoods. They delighted in being profane and shocking as if to demonstrate the vitality and strength of black activism. Members of the Black Arts movement often considered themselves revolutionaries, supporting both peaceful and violent forms of protest. They saw their role as artists to do more than just create; they needed to agitate, to be active in order to reach their political goals.

THE LITERARY CRITICISM OF HENRY LOUIS GATES, JR.

When Gates began studying literary theory and criticism at Cambridge, he concentrated his studies on African American writing of the eighteenth century. In addition, Gates was encouraged to apply more contemporary literary theories to his examination of these early black writings. What Gates was hoping to learn was whether African American literature could be studied, analyzed, and explained using these contemporary methods that were commonly used on English literature. These "experiments" in literary criticism turned out to be a powerful tool for Gates, as they provided the foundation for much of his later writings on black literature and literary criticism and theory.[14]

Gates was the only black student on the Cambridge campus; in fact, it was said that he was also the first black student at Cambridge ever that anyone could remember. This isolation led to him personalize his studies and interpretation of the black literature he was examining in a way that might not have been possible had he been back at Yale. He approached the texts in a very personal way; what were these words trying to say to him as an African American living in a racist society?[15]

In the course of his studies, Gates also felt compelled to study these texts in this manner as a way of meeting a challenge "for the race" just as W. E. B. Du Bois had done with his studies in sociology. Gates recalled that he felt as if he had "embarked upon a mission for all black people," but most especially for black scholars who traditionally have been called "race men" whose job it is to "collect, preserve, and analyze" the "artifacts of the black imagination." Gates also found in studying literary theory that racism was inherent. The different schools of thought that exist in literary theory and criticism are all considered to be part of what is known as the "Western canon" or traditions that reflect analysis from the perspective of being white, male, and Western (European).[16]

Through the reading of his texts, Gates would develop a brand-new form of literary criticism, one that allowed the reading of African American and other black texts with an eye to the black tradition of literature. This meant that black writings would be studied in the context of the black experience instead of being analyzed according to the prevailing tenets of Western literary traditions. Studying black texts within black culture then allowed contemporary literary theories to help explain and make these writings more meaningful and significant for the reader.

Gates was particularly fascinated with black language. To him, it is the language that makes black writing so unique within the larger world of literature. He later wrote, "Much of my work in black criticism arises from my analysis of the racist uses to which the absence of black writing has been put since the eighteenth century." Gates also realized that as black writers defended themselves against racism, they could only do so within the confines of the Western literary tradition, leading them to accept this standard that at the same time rejected them as people and as writers.[17]

Even as he developed this new way of looking at black literature, Gates was in no hurry to demolish the older, established Western tradition. In later interviews, Gates went to great lengths to explain his views:

> Now, I wouldn't want to get rid of anything in that tradition. I think the Western tradition has been a marvelous, wonderful tradition. But it's not the only tradition full of great ideas. And I'm not talking about any diminishment of standards. Even by the most conservative notion of what is good and bad, we will find excellence in other cultures, like the great Indian cultures, the great Chinese cultures, the great African cultures.[18]

For Gates, the idea is to have not two separate literary traditions but a true intermingling of those traditions. To achieve that would bring American literature a true plurality, which is in keeping with the truest essence of what America, as a diverse and rich country, is all about. To that end, Gates would work throughout his career to promote those very ideals.

NOTES

1. Lindsay Patterson, *International Library of African American Life and History: An Introduction to Black Literature in American, from 1746 to the Present* (New York: The Association for the Study of Afro-American life and History, 1978), 25.

2. Ondra Krouse Dismukes, "African American Literature: An Overview," *Gale Library of Daily Life: Slavery and America.* Orville Vernon Burton, ed. Vol. 2 (Detroit: Gale, 2008), 187–190. Gale U.S. History in Context. Web. August 21, 2010; Arnold Rampersad and Stefanie Dunning, "Literature of the United States." *Encyclopedia of African-American Culture and History*. Colin A. Palmer, ed. 2nd ed. Vol. 3. (Detroit: Macmillan Reference USA, 2006), 1323–1333. Gale U.S. History in Context. Web. August 21, 2010; "The African-American Literary Experience," *The African-American Experience* (Woodbridge, CT: Primary Source Media, 1999). American Journey. Gale U.S. History in Context. Web. August 25, 2010.

3. Rampersad and Dunning, "Literature of the United States," 1323–1333.

4. Ibid.

5. Ibid.

6. Ibid.

7. "The African-American Literary Experience."

8. Ibid.; Rampersad and Dunning, "Literature of the United States," 1323–1333.

9. Rampersad and Dunning, "Literature of the United States," 1323–1333.

10. Ibid.

11. "The African-American Literary Experience."

12. Ibid.

13. Ibid.

14. Henry Louis Gates, Jr., *Figures in Black: Words, Signs, and the "Racial" Self* (New York: Oxford University Press, 1987), xvi–xvii.

15. Ibid., xvii.

16. Ibid.

17. Ibid., xvii–xviii.

18. Breena Clarke and Susan Tifft, "A Race Man Argues for a Broader Curriculum: Henry Louis Gates, Jr.," *Time*, April 22, 1991, http://www.time.com/time/magazine/article/0,9171,972763,00.html.

Chapter 7

THE LITERARY ARCHAEOLOGIST

In 1979, Henry Louis Gates, Jr. became the first African American to receive a Ph.D. from the venerable 800-year-old British institution Cambridge University. It had been a long road for Gates, but one filled with rich experiences. Upon receiving his degree, Gates returned to Yale, where he joined the faculty as an assistant professor, teaching in both the English and African American Studies departments.

Still, Gates realized upon his return from England that the state of African American studies was in flux. As he later recounted in an interview, "There were very real worries that Afro-American studies—because of its origins as an appeasement for political demands, by and large, throughout the academy—would not survive. Many cynical administrators set it up so it wouldn't survive." Fortunately, because of the dedication of scholars such as African American historian John Blassingame and historian Charles T. Davis, who was also head of the African American studies program, the field was surviving. Even though Gates had other options that he could pursue, he believed that by coming to Yale, particularly with Charles Davis as his mentor, not only would he eventually get tenure, which would allow him to stay at the university as long as he wanted, but that he would also in time, assume the leadership of the African American studies program.[1]

SETTLING IN

Besides his keen intellect and thirst for knowledge, Henry Louis Gates at the age of 29 possessed a charisma and self-assurance that could not help but guarantee him a good chance at academic success. Clearly, Gates was quite comfortable moving between the white and black worlds. Perhaps more important, as one journalist described him, "he made white people comfortable in his." At the time Gates returned to Yale, African American militants were still very much a part of the American political, social, and cultural landscape. Many whites viewed them with fear and distaste. But Gates had no such allegiances, his interests being literature and history instead of politics and public policy, which allowed him to avoid the kinds of confrontations that seemed almost inevitable in that current political climate. Instead, Gates was choosing to immerse himself in an arena that was known to be brutal and petty: the world of academics.[2]

As Gates was settling into his new job, he took time to legally formalize his relationship with Sharon. After living together for seven years, the two were married in 1979 at his brother Rocky's house in New Jersey. Still, it was an important step for the couple, given the initial problems they had faced with Sharon's family. "My father could never say, 'I'm a racist and I hate Skip,'" Sharon said in a 2009 interview, "But he could say, 'I'm a Baptist and you're living in sin, so I hate you both.'" The couple soon became parents of two daughters: Maggie in July 1980 and Liza in January 1982.[3]

Gates almost immediately set out to make his mark in the world of academe. The year 1979 not only marked his receiving his Ph.D., it also saw the publication of three articles: "Dis and Dat: Dialect and the Descent," "Figures in Black: Words, Signs, and the 'Racial' Self," and "Preface to Blackness: Text and Pretext." All three publications paved the way for much of Gates's later work on African American literature and literary theory. This early work also earned Gates the first of many grants, this time from the National Endowment for the Humanities.[4]

By this time, Gates had developed close working relationships with a number of scholars on the Yale faculty. Along with historian John Blassingame, historian William McFeeley, who had won a Pulitzer Prize for his biographical work on Ulysses S. Grant, George Steiner, a literary critic, and Wole Soyinka joined Gates for breakfast most every morning at a local restaurant, the Naples Pizza Shop, where the group discussed their work and research. For Gates, the meetings were another way to try out his ideas and solicit feedback for his work. This "rainbow coalition of mentors" was invaluable to Gates as he continued his research work. In an interview about Gates, John Blassingame, then chairman of the African American Studies department, called the meetings "sounding boards for all kinds of wild ideas that we have. We [Gates and Blassingame] both regularly stop by there, at about the same time." Other members of the department would often join the discussions, which ranged from insightful to uproarious, but always interesting.[5]

"THE GENIUS AWARD"

One of the most prestigious grants awarded in the United States is the MacArthur Fellows Program or MacArthur Fellowship, which has also been nicknamed the Genius Award. The grant is an annual award given out by the MacArthur Foundation, which was established by the John D. and Catherine T. MacArthur Foundation. John D. MacArthur was a very successful businessman who created the Bankers Life and Casualty Company, as well as a host of other businesses. He also owned a large amount of real estate properties in Florida and New York. His wife Catherine was a successful businesswoman who held positions in many of her husband's companies; she also served as a director of the Foundation.

According to the Foundation's website, "the fellowship is not a reward for past accomplishment, but rather an investment in a person's originality, insight, and potential." Each year, anywhere between 20 and 40 U.S. citizens who "show exceptional merit and promise for continued and enhanced creative work" are given a MacArthur Grant. The award pays out a total of $500,000, paid as quarterly installments over five years. The recipients of the award can be from any discipline or field of study; there is no age limit or any other restrictions.

Unlike other awards, though, the MacArthur Fellowship has no application. Colleagues who submit recommendations to a small selection committee nominate people anonymously. The committee, which numbers about a dozen people, is also anonymous. This committee reviews each nominee and then passes along its recommendations to the MacArthur Foundation's president and the board of directors. In the majority of cases, most MacArthur Fellows first learn that they have even been considered when they receive the congratulatory phone call telling them they have won an award.[6]

In 1981, the MacArthur Foundation awarded its first "genius grants" to 21 individuals. Among the winners was Henry Louis Gates, Jr., at that point an assistant professor at Yale. Gates recalled that a man called on the telephone and announced that Gates was to receive $30,000 a year for five years with no strings attached. Gates did not believe what he was hearing and told his caller to "quit fooling." However, the next morning, Gates was standing by the gates of the university. He was still unconvinced, yet he waited to see if a messenger came with the letter of confirmation. "Embarrassed by his own eagerness," Gates took the letter and went back to his apartment, where he learned that he had indeed won one of the coveted MacArthur Foundation grants. The prize money came at a critical point for Gates, for it now allowed him the "financial and psychological freedom to pursue more obscure areas of literary theory." To celebrate, Gates ran out and bought a coveted collection of videos from the old *Amos and Andy* TV series, which he and his father had so enjoyed when he was growing up.[7]

One of the first projects that Gates undertook with the award monies was the Black Periodical Literature Project, an endeavor talked about by Gates and John Blassingame over their breakfasts at the Naples. At that time, Blassingame was trying to annotate Frederick Douglass's speeches and was using black newspapers. Gates, as well as other African American scholars, knew there existed hundreds and hundreds of black newspapers and magazines in the nineteenth century, but there was no easy way to track these resources down. Blassingame encouraged Gates, along with Charles T. Davis, to investigate the texts, and the three founded the Black Periodical Fiction Project. With the help of funding from the National Endowment for the Humanities, the Black Periodical Literature Project would restore thousands of black authors to visibility within American and African American literature.

Gates, working alongside one of his mentors, Charles T. Davis, helped collect and annotate a large collection of African American periodicals, including books, newspapers, and magazine articles. Over time, the project would move with Gates. Eventually, he and his staff would catalogue thousands of pieces of literature authored by African Americans, including 12,000 works of short fiction, 18,000 poems and 42,000 book reviews and literary notices from 1827 to 1940.[8]

OUR NIG

Later that year, Gates was perusing books in a rare-book store in Manhattan. A small, worn-looking volume caught his eye; the book was dated 1859 and titled *Our Nig: or, Sketches From the Life of a Free Black in A Two-Story White House, North. Showing That Slavery's Shadows Fall Even There*. The author was an H. E. Wilson. Gates stopped to take a look at the book, not because he had ever heard of the book, but rather, as he later stated, "It was the first book I know of which used the word 'nigger' or a derivative of it before the Civil War." Gates went ahead and bought the book for $50. He later said, "When I bought it, I assumed it was written by a white person about blacks during the middle of the nineteenth century and that it was one more fantasy like *Gone with the Wind* with darkies strumming the banjos out in the field." Still, the book sat on his shelf for well over a year before he decided to take a more serious look at it.[9]

Gates was well aware that a few bibliographies and literary histories included Wilson's novel. But in all cases, the book's author was identified as being either a white man or woman or gave no indication at all of the author's race. But Gates observed early on that the preface to the novel read like the words of a black woman. Further, at the end of the novel were three letters of endorsement, written by whites. To help get their works published, African American writers used such letters. For the next six months, Gates researched the book and its author. Gates then realized what an exciting discovery he had made: *Our Nig* was the first novel in the United States published by an African American woman named Harriet Wilson.[10]

Wilson's *Our Nig* is a curious kind of book, detailing the life of an indentured northern black woman in the mid-nineteenth century, and is based on the life of Wilson. The character, Frado, is an unusual one for the literary times as well: she is the product of a mixed marriage, which was taboo during that period. Frado is abandoned by her mother and becomes an indentured servant to a white Boston family at the age of six. During her servitude, she is abused, physically and mentally. Upon her eighteenth birthday, Frado is freed. She then marries a black man who poses as a fugitive slave and earns money by giving lectures on his so-called "experiences" as a runaway slave. When Frado becomes pregnant, her husband abandons her and the baby. When her son contracts fever, Frado is forced to put him in the poorhouse. The author's motive in writing the novel is made plain at the end, when she appeals to the reader to buy her book so that she can free her son.

For Gates, the book became a personal journey of discovery after his first reading. One of the first things bothering Gates was the perception that the book initially was written by a white man. In the preface to *Our Nig*, the author states that she was black and was appealing to "my colored brethren universally for patronage."[11] As far as Gates was concerned, "There was no reason for a white person to pretend he or she was black in those days."[12] Determined to know more about Wilson, Gates began looking through documents throughout the East Coast, looking at census data and old newspapers and magazines. He finally centered his search in Boston, where the book was originally printed.

Then one day, while looking through the Boston City Directory, Gates found an H. E. Wilson living in a neighborhood known as Robinson Alley. Unfortunately, when he searched through a microfilm of the 1860 census, the information for that neighborhood was missing. Gates then concentrated his efforts, going through the yellowed and decaying pages of the original Boston City Directory at the state archives. After looking through hundreds of pages, the Robinson Alley portion of the census, which had been tucked behind one of the pages, fell out. Located next to Harriet E. Wilson's name was a large letter "B," which noted that Wilson was black.[13]

Convinced that he had found the author, Gates then tried to locate the son who was mentioned in the appendix of the book. Finally, one of Gates's colleagues found a death certificate for George Mason Wilson, son of "Mrs. H. E. Wilson," the name that appears on the copyright page of *Our Nig*. For Gates, this was the last piece of the puzzle. He had found not only the author but also her son. Unfortunately, he later learned that Wilson's son died at the age of seven, only six months after his mother's book was published.[14]

Gates's discovery was an important one. Previously, literary scholars believed that the first novel published in the United States by an African American was William Wells Brown's novel *Clotelle*, which had been published in four different versions between 1853 and 1867. Gates's unearthing of the work also proved important to the study of African American literature by extending the scope of the African American woman's literary tradition by more than 30 years. Gates believed that there were three primary reasons that Wilson's book was overlooked for so many years. First, the novel explores themes that in the mid-nineteenth century North, abolitionists and free blacks could not afford to have made public, namely that racism was alive and well in the north, that a black man would pose as an ex-slave to earn money, and that interracial marriages existed.

For Gates, the discovery of Wilson's novel fulfilled what he later called his "Christopher Columbus" complex. After a *New York Times* article detailed Gates's discovery, publishers bid furiously for the rights to reprint *Our Nig*, with Random House eventually winning the bidding war. Gates would also serve as the volume's editor. Even upon its publication, Gates was amazed at his discovery, stating that "So many wonderful people have uncovered so much authentic material out of the cracks of Afro-American literary history, that I couldn't quite believe that such a gold mine could have remained uncovered."[15]

TRANSITIONS AND *TRANSITION*

From 1979 until 1984, Gates continued to teach at Yale University, splitting his time between the English and African American Studies departments. Besides teaching a full load at the university, Gates was also busy with his wife raising two daughters, as well as working on four books in various stages of prepublication. However, in 1985, Gates was turned down for tenure at the university.

To some, it appeared that Gates was paying the price for the increasingly high visibility he had attained in the last few years. His recent fame, due to the publication of *Our Nig*, had not only thrust him and his family into the spotlight but had also garnered him hate mail, in part because of his marriage to a white woman. Some in the Yale faculty and administration viewed Gates as a "flashy careerist" instead of a more dignified, quiet, and refined professor. The former began to be a real problem for Gates, especially after the untimely death of his mentor, Charles Davis, from cancer. With the loss of Blassingame and Davis, Gates really had no one to champion him or his research.[16]

In 1985, when Gates came up for tenure in the English department, he lost out the position to literary critic Robert Stepto. Gates was devastated and resigned immediately, his dream apparently shattered. "My whole intellectual life was dependent upon the expectation that I would get tenure at Yale," he stated in a 2009 interview.

> It was meant to be an insult. I was hurt. I felt like I had let Charles Davis down. I lived and breathed African American studies through him. I gave the eulogy at his funeral. I wept at his grave. I loved Charles. I'd always thought he would live a long time, and we were going to raise our families together. That was the plan. I felt like I'd been hit in the stomach.[17]

Gates then accepted an offer to teach as a full professor in the English and Africana Studies departments at Cornell University in Ithaca, New York. Joining Gates was his friend and colleague Kwame Appiah, who, even though he had received tenure at Yale, resigned to join his friend at Cornell. Gates appreciated the gesture of his friend, stating later, "It was a courageous statement [for him to leave]. Without him, I don't know if I would've made it. We still held out this dream that somewhere, some way we would build a department."[18]

But Gates soon realized that he would be unable to create the kind of African American studies department that he had dreamed of.

Instead, he, Appiah, and a Yale senior, Henry Finder, got together to revive the magazine *Transition*, which focused on black culture and politics, and which had been founded in Uganda in 1961. Gates's mentor and friend Wole Soyinka had edited it in the 1970s, with Gates serving as the American editor. However, the money ran out and the magazine ceased to exist. Gates was able to revive the magazine with Soyinka serving as chairman of the editorial board, Appiah and Gates as editors, and Finder as managing editor.[19]

In 1988 Gates was named the W. E. B. Du Bois Professor of Literature, becoming the first African American male to hold an endowed chair in the history of Cornell University. On top of the promotion, Cornell provided resources, including staff, working space, and additional financial help for Gates to pursue the numerous projects he was working on, including the Black Periodical Literature Project.

THE SIGNIFYIN(G) MONKEY

In 1987, *Figures in Black: Words, Signs, and the "Racial" Self*, a collection of previously published essays and articles, was published. The book set the stage for much of Gates's future works. In his essays, Gates contended that standard literary theories that traditionally have been drawn from the Western literary tradition were inadequate when studying the literature of African Americans. To demonstrate the problem, Gates chose many essays that reflected on a particular piece of African American literature and applied contemporary critical methods to interpret them.

According to Gates, the black literary tradition was unique: "Unlike almost every other literary tradition," he writes in *Figures in Black*, "the Afro-American literary tradition was generated as a response to eighteenth- and nineteenth-century allegations that persons of African descent did not, and could not, create literature." For Gates, one way to define the African American literary tradition is to view it apart from Western or European influences. His approach in segregating black literature has been called "racist, separatist, nationalist or essentialist."[20]

Even as Gates was making a name for himself, he was burdened with sad news. In April 1987, Gates's mother, Pauline, died of a heart attack. His father decided to come and live with Gates and his family. Gates grieved for his mother deeply. "The clichéd thing to say is that it makes you aware of the transitory nature of all human relationships," he said many years later. "But it made me a fanatically loyal person. In the end you only have a handful of real relationships, and I am fanatical about those relationships. I take a long time before I trust someone enough to want them in my world or to be in their world. And once they are there, I don't want them to go."[21]

Following on the heels of *Figures in Black* came Gates's next book, *The Signifyin(g) Monkey: Towards a Theory of Afro-American Literary Criticism*, published in 1988. In *The Signifyin(g) Monkey*, Gates defined his literary approach further in the critiquing of African American literature using a separate cultural criteria. As he states in his Preface, "The challenge of my project, if not exactly to invent a black theory, was to locate and identify how the 'black tradition' had theorized about itself." Using the work of other scholars who have studied African American literature, Gates theorized that to understand the black literary "canon," or standard, one must look to the African roots that have been passed down through generations of African American history and culture.[22]

The very title of his book demonstrates one aspect of Gates's thinking: to signify, which is a form of black vernacular speech. In the black vernacular, signifying is a sign that words cannot be trusted, that even the most literal utterance allows room for interpretation. When the first slaves were brought to America, many resisted learning the language of their white masters. Instead, they created their own language or vernacular. By placing the letter "g" in parentheses, Gates is essentially "signifyin." For him, to understand black literature, one must understand the African American vernacular language in which words can have double meanings, that is, one meaning according to blacks and another meaning according to whites. Gates describes various African myths and African American literature and then attempts to link them through this vernacular tradition. For Gates then, the action of "signifyin(g)" is the equivalent of a ritual language that functions almost as a source of double speak that links African and African American literary texts.[23]

The book begins with a chapter on an African mythological figure known as Esu-Elegbara. There then follows a chapter in which Gates explains what the Signifying Monkey is and how it relates to black English vernacular. According to Gates, there exists an entire series of African oral narrative poems about the "signifying monkey." Even though the retelling of the story can differ, the general outline is as follows. In the jungle, the lion claims to be king, even though everyone knows that the real king is the elephant. The monkey, tired of the lion's roaring and posturing, insults the lion publicly. When the lion becomes angry, the monkey shrugs and states that he is merely repeating what the elephant has been saying all along. The lion, angered at having his supremacy challenged, confronts the elephant, who beats him.

Some versions of the story have the monkey succeeding with his deception; others do not. But in any case, the monkey has been successful in "signifying." The tale continued to be told among the slaves once in America, as well as having become a standard story in African American culture. For Gates, the concept of signifying stands as a "discrete black difference" in African American literature. For instance, many African American writers have "signified upon" earlier writers, or imitated them, but with a different intent in mind.[24]

Gates tried out his theory in the second half of the book, which consists of close readings of different texts, spanning several centuries of African American literature. These texts included four different slave narratives written between 1774 and 1830, Zora Neale Hurston's 1937 work *Their Eyes Were Watching God*, Ishmael Reed's 1972 novel *Mumbo Jumbo*, and finally Alice Walker's 1982 novel *The Color Purple*. Gates also discusses other African American writers such as W. E. B. Du Bois, Jean Toomer, Richard Wright, and Ralph Ellison.

With his books *Figures in Black* and *The Signifyin(g) Monkey*, Gates undertook a bold new approach, not only creating a new form of literary criticism for African American literature that linked both black texts and traditions specifically but also changing the manner in which African American literature would be studied. The culmination of his years at Yale, then Cambridge, in pursuit of understanding the African American literary tradition all came together in these writings. With the swoop of his pen, Gates refused to accept any further the conventional and pre-existing assumptions about African

American literature. By utilizing contemporary methods of analyzing literature, Gates took African American literature and stood it on its head. No longer did one have to accept the prevailing view that the majority of black writing was steeped in social realism. This notion in particular, of Afro-American literature as social realism, was in effect rejected by Gates.[25]

Gates's book and literary theories generated a firestorm of controversy. Some critics, such as D. G. Myers, charged that Gates was taking a giant leap in presupposing that all African American authors are "signifying" in responding to each other's texts and works. In his review for *The New Republic*, Andrew Delbanco, a Columbia University professor, argued that much of *The Signifying Monkey* is obscured by the jargon of contemporary literary criticism, a "hermetic language" that subverts Gates's true inclination, which is "to meet the texts on their own terms."[26]

Other literary critics such as Stanley Fish strongly supported Gates's efforts by stating that in his application of a new kind of language for literary theory, whether it is a slave narrative or a current work of African American fiction, Gates has earned "legitimacy for African American literature that it shouldn't need to prove." Sacvan Bercovitch, a professor of English at Harvard, responded that Gates has "found a way of asserting the existence of a separate black American tradition, and of asserting this in a way that places the black American tradition at the cutting edge of literary theory." The idea, too, that "many skeptics believe that Gates has merely found a gimmick" was, for Bercovitch, ludicrous.[27]

Despite its controversial stance, *The Signifyin(g) Monkey* earned Gates an American Book Award in 1999, as well as increased exposure in both academic and popular magazines and newspapers. Gates continued to work on numerous projects, including book reviews, magazine articles, and his own books. For both his critics and supporters, it was becoming clear that Henry Louis Gates, Jr., was becoming a name to be reckoned with in the field of literature and literary criticism.

THE LITERARY ARCHAEOLOGIST

By the close of the 1980s, Henry Louis Gates, Jr., was being referred to as a "literary archaeologist" for his abilities at unearthing overlooked or forgotten texts of African American literature. In 1988, the prodigious 30-volume set of books focusing on African American women writers was released: *The Schomburg Library of Nineteenth-Century Black Women Writers.*

The project had its early beginnings, again, with the late historian John Blassingame. In 1980, when the Black Periodical Literature Project first got underway at Yale University, Gates and Blassingame began uncovering the written works, including fiction and poetry, of several nineteenth-century African American women writers. Blassingame was in the midst of preparing an index of letters to the editor in antislavery periodicals when he discovered a number of the texts. During the course of the project, Gates discovered that almost 40 percent of the writings uncovered had been written by women.

Gates understood the importance of such a discovery for both American and African American literary history. "When I looked up the books mentioned in those reviews, they weren't listed in any of the standard bibliographies of black literature," Gates said in a 1988 telephone interview. Gates recognized that although studies of African American literature had acknowledged the work of some women, many were still overlooked or forgotten. Coupled with that was the attitude of African American men of the time, such as abolitionist Frederick Douglass, who when in 1892 was asked to name some black women for inclusion in a reference book, remarked, "I have thus far seen no book of importance written by a Negro woman." To uncover these writings, Gates photocopied bibliographies and checked research libraries such as the Schomburg Center for Research in Black Culture, which is a division of the New York Public Library. The Schomburg Center houses one of the world's largest collections of information about African Americans. Gates also visited the Moreland-Spingarn Collection at Howard University and the Boston Public Library.[28]

After putting together his own bibliography, Gates now had to track down the works. He discovered that many had never been reprinted; several copies could be found only in research libraries, making them almost impossible to view. Some were so rare, they could not be shipped for viewing, nor could they be photocopied because of their fragile nature. Gates also had to check to make sure that the books were actually written by black women, not white women or men. In the end, Gates had a list that included 45 books, written by black women, which eventually allowed him to create "a library of the Afro-American woman's mind."[29]

Gates then contacted Oxford University Press and began organizing what would become the Schomburg Library. In addition to working with the press, Gates also contacted the center, which provided Gates with enough material from its rare book collection for 24 of the first 30 volumes, focusing on the period between 1890 and 1910, in which there was an extraordinary output of African American women's writing. Gates then drew on the talents and expertise of scholars across the country to edit the works and write introductions to each volume of the series. The works included seven volumes of fiction, three volumes of essays, 11 volumes of biographies, and nine books of poetry, including "The Collected Works of Phillis Wheatley," who is considered the "symbolic mother of the black female literary tradition."

Other works in the series included *The Journal of Charlotte Forten*, a diary kept by a free black woman who lived on the islands off Georgia in the decade just before the Civil War, and *Iola Le Roy*, an 1892 novel about slavery and Reconstruction by Frances Harper, who is thought to be the first black woman to make a living from her writing. *A Voice from the South*, also published in 1892, is a collection of essays by Anna Julia Cooper, an early black feminist. Other titles included Ann Plato's *Essays* and Emma Dunham Kelley's novel *Megda*, and *Four Girls at Cottage City*. Gates dedicated the series to his mother for inspiring him to his love of learning and of literature. The series would eventually spawn a 10-volume supplement in 1991.[30]

In the foreword to the series, Gates wrote, "Until now it has been extraordinarily difficult to establish the formal connections between early black women's writing and that of the present, precisely because our knowledge of their work has been broken and sporadic." Further, Gates declared that without acknowledging and publishing these writings, "a significant segment of the black tradition" would have "remain[ed] silent."[31]

Gates makes an eloquent argument as to the literary, social, and cultural importance of these writings. "Throughout these books, the women made it clear that they needed 'to be allowed to speak for themselves,'" rather than having black men try to speak for and about them. Gates points out that in 1773, Phillis Wheatley's *Poems* commenced two vital literary traditions at once: the African American literary tradition and the African American women's literary tradition. That alone makes her accomplishments—and those of her fellow writers—even more extraordinary in the history of American literature. Gates also recognized that black women writers were among the first to move beyond other literary forms, utilizing the essay and novel as a means of conveying their thoughts.[32]

Overall, the response to the collection was extremely favorable, with historians, literary critics, and literary historians applauding Gates's efforts at successfully completing such a daunting project. Still, there were critics, many of whom questioned why a male editor was chosen for the project instead of a female. But several of the leading female academics that contributed introductory essays to the project had no complaints, citing Gates's abilities and tenacity at uncovering and bringing attention to long-forgotten works of black literature. In addition, the success of the Schomburg Library seemed to further cement Gates's reputation as a literary scholar and "literary archaeologist."[33]

As a result, his rising star and the scarcity of black scholars in the academic world put Gates's abilities and services at a premium. He was flooded with offers to come and teach at such prestigious institutions as Columbia University in New York City and Stanford University in California. Cornell, afraid at the possibility of losing him, gave Gates unprecedented authority to hire new African American faculty members for the department. In addition, Gates now enjoyed other fruits of his success, such as a New York literary agent and a new Mercedes Benz automobile. It was clear that not only was he becoming a big name in academics, his popularity was setting the archetype for a new kind of figure in academia: the "academic superstar." Finally, in 1990, after more than two years of negotiations, Gates made a decision about the next, new direction for his life and career: he decided to move his family to Durham, North Carolina, where he would attempt to resuscitate the African American Studies program at Duke University.[34]

NOTES

1. Bruce Cole, "Interview: Henry Louis Gates," 2002, http://www.neh.gov/whoweare/gates/interview.html.

2. Cheryl Bentsen, "Head Negro in Charge," *Boston Magazine*, July 23, 2009, http://www.bostonmagazine.com/articles/Henry_Louis_Gates_Jr/page5

3. Ibid.

4. Henry Louis Gates, "Dis and Dat: Dialect and the Descent," *Afro-American Literature: The Reconstruction of Instruction*, Robert Stepto and Dexter Fisher, eds. (New York: Modern Language Association, 1979), 88–121; Henry Louis Gates, Jr., *Figures in Black: Words, Signs, and the "Racial" Self* (Oxford: Oxford University Press, 1987), 167–195; "Preface to Blackness: Text and Pretext," *Afro-American Literature: The Reconstruction of Instruction*. Robert Stepto and Dexter Fisher, eds. (New York: Modern Language Association, 1979), 44–71.

5. Bruce Cole, "Interview: Henry Louis Gates," 2002, http://www.neh.gov/whoweare/gates/interview.html; Elizabeth Alexander, "Pursuing the Pages of History; Yale's Henry Louis Gates & the Roots of Black Literature, "*Washington Post*, August 10, 1983, B1.

6. MacArthur Foundation, http://www.macfound.org/site/c.lkLXJ8MQKrH/b.855245/k.588/About_the_Foundation.htm.

7. Adam Begley, "Black Studies' New Star: Henry Louis Gates Jr.," *The New York Times*, April 1, 1990, http://www.nytimes.com/1990/04/01/magazine/black-studies-new-star-henry-louis-gates-jr.html?pagewanted=4; Joyce Wansley, "With the discovery of Our Nig, Henry Gates becomes the Sherlock Holmes of black studies," *People Weekly*, September 12, 1983: 115+. General OneFile. Web. September 13, 2010.

8. Mary Lou Beatty, "Biography: Henry Louis Gates, Jr.," http://www.neh.gov/whoweare/gates/biography.html.

9. Michelle Slung, "Book World," *Washington Post*, May 18, 1983, 23; Joyce Wansley, "With the discovery of Our Nig, Henry Gates becomes the Sherlock Holmes of black studies."

10. Joyce Wansley, "With the discovery of Our Nig, Henry Gates becomes the Sherlock Holmes of black studies."

11. H. E. Wilson, *Our Nig: Or, Sketches From the Life of a Free Black* (New York: Random House Publishers), n.p., 2011.

12. Joyce Wansley, "With the discovery of Our Nig, Henry Gates becomes the Sherlock Holmes of black studies."

13. Scott Thompson, "Discovery of oldest US novel by black author adds page to history books," *Christian Science Monitor*, April 12, 1983, 1.

14. Ibid.

15. Joyce Wansley, "With the discovery of Our Nig, Henry Gates becomes the Sherlock Holmes of black studies"; Scott Thompson, "Discovery of oldest US novel by black author adds page to history books."

16. Cheryl Bentsen, "Head Negro in Charge," *Boston Magazine*, July 23, 2009, http://www.bostonmagazine.com/articles/Henry_Louis_Gates_Jr/page5.

17. Ibid.

18. Ibid.

19. Ibid.

20. Henry Louis Gates, *Figures in Black: Words, Signs and the "Racial" Self* (New York: Oxford University Press, 1989), 25.

21. Cheryl Bentsen, "Head Negro in Charge," 6.

22. Henry Louis Gates, *The Signifyin(g) Monkey* (New York: Oxford University Press, 1988), ix.

23. John Wideman, "Playing, Not Joking with Language," *The New York Times*, August 14, 1988, Section 7, 3.

24. Henry Louis Gates, *The Signifyin(g) Monkey*, xxiv, 81, 88; D. G. Myers, "Signifying Nothing," *New Criterion* 8 (February 1990): 61–64.

25. James Olney, "Henry Louis Gates, Jr." *Modern American Critics Since 1955*. Ed. Gregory S. Jay. Detroit: Gale Research, 1988. *Dictionary of Literary Biography* Vol. 67. Literature Resource Center. Web. September 16, 2010.

26. Andrew Delbanco, "The Signifying Monkey: A Theory of Afro-American Literary Criticism," *The New Republic*, January 9, 1989: 28+. General OneFile. Web. September 14, 2010; D. G. Myers, "Signifying Nothing," *New Criterion* 8 (February 1990): 61–64.

27. Andrew Delbanco, "The Signifying Monkey: A Theory of Afro-American Literary Criticism"; D. G. Myers, "Signifying Nothing," *New Criterion* 8 (February 1990): 61–64; Adam Begley, "Black Studies New Star: Henry Louis Gates, Jr.," *The New York Times*, April 1, 1990, http://www.nytimes.com/1990/04/01/magazine/black-studies-new-star-henry-louis-gates-jr.html?

28. C. Gerald Fraser, "A Scholar Traces 'Lost' Literature of Black Women in America," *The New York Times*, April 21, 1988, Section C, 23.

29. Ibid.

30. Eric J. Sundquist, "A Great American Flowering (Book Review Desk)," *The New York Times Book Review*, July 3, 1988. General Reference Center Gold. Web. September 14, 2010.

31. Henry Louis Gates, *The Schomburg Library of Nineteenth-Century Black Women Writers* (New York: Oxford University Press, 1988), xi, xxii.

32. C. Gerald Fraser, "A Scholar Traces 'Lost' Literature of Black Women in America," *The New York Times*, April 21, 1988, Section C, 23; Jean Fagan Yellin, "Women Who Made a Difference," *The Washington Post*, April 10, 1988, X1.

33. Mary B. W. Tabor, "Echoes of Voices Long Silent—Black Women Writers Rediscovered," *Christian Science Monitor*, February 25, 1988, 19.

34. Cheryl Bentsen, "Head Negro in Charge," *Boston Magazine*, July 23, 2009, http://www.bostonmagazine.com/articles/Henry_Louis_Gates_Jr/page6.

Chapter 8

BUILDING A DREAM

Once again, Gates was presented with the opportunity to build the African American Studies department he envisioned. Sweetening the deal to move to Duke University was the assurance that he could bring his friend Kwame Appiah, who was offered a position in the philosophy department, as well as Henry Finder and *Transition* magazine. The Black Periodical Literature Project begun at Yale and continued at Cornell would also have a new home at Duke. The university also hoped with Gates's help to hire Wole Soyinka. Rumors persisted that the dean of the college of arts and sciences at Duke was preparing a list of black scholars who might be attracted to Duke now that Gates was teaching there. In addition, the Duke administration pledged to spend several hundred thousand dollars over the next few years to revitalize the African American Studies program. As one professor commented, "We have a lot of hopes pinned on Skip Gates."[1] Although not without precedent, the agreement that a newly hired professor can make additional hiring decisions is rare. It was a sign of Gates's rising status and power.[2]

The hiring of Henry Louis Gates, Jr. also reflected a growing trend among academic institutions and African American scholars. By the

1990s, the number of African American college students had declined, as had the number of blacks earning doctorates. Gates represented that generation of African American academics who came of age during the 1960s, a time when many of the elite universities in America opened their doors to minority students as well as establishing black studies programs. Now there was concern about where the next generation of black scholars would come from. Duke administrators not only saw in Gates the opportunity to bring an academic superstar to their campus but also hoped that with Gates in residence, they could attract additional African American students and faculty.

THE FOUNDERING OF AFRICAN AMERICAN STUDIES

By the 1990s, the African American studies departments and programs on most American college campuses had seen better days. Many had fallen into disarray; others had ceased to exist. From its heyday as a coherent discipline in the 1960s and 1970s, the field had become spread out among many departments. Its course offerings were diverse, unfocused, often highly specialized, and sometimes intellectually suspect. Many faculty members were poorly trained. On numerous campuses, African American studies had become a joke. Students, white and black, took such courses because they felt assured of receiving an easy A. More thoughtful students, again both black and white, had contempt for a program that they thought diluted the quality of their educations.

As a result, black studies fell into a long decline; those departments that still survived were noted far more for their outrageous pronouncements than their careful scholarship. Leonard Jeffries, the chairman of the Black Studies Program at City College of New York, became notorious for his attacks on Jews and his theory classifying blacks as "sun people" and whites as "ice people," meaning that blacks by nature were warm and loving and whites by nature cold and unfeeling. Other Afrocentrists argued, and set out to prove, that all culture had come from Africa. The ancient Egyptians, they asserted, had invented the first airplanes and discovered electricity.[3] Europeans had oppressed Africans, appropriated their cultural and technological achievements, and then engaged in a vast conspiracy to rewrite history to claim these accomplishments for themselves and to divest Africans of their heritage and their birthright.

Another of the problems facing African American studies programs across the country were the charges leveled by conservative academics who believed such programs lacked rigor, that the eclectic offerings that constituted most African American studies programs did not qualify the field as an independent discipline. Instead, courses with an African American element should be offered within their respective departments, African American history in a history department, African American literature in an English Department, and so on. Advocates of this position explained that by offering these courses within the context of their disciplines, the subject stood a better chance of being taught with greater rigor and thereby earning greater respect and acceptance. Many other scholars, including Gates, disagreed. Maintaining autonomous black studies programs and identifying black studies as an independent discipline, he thought, was vital if it were to survive.

This growing conflict was not just about the validity of African American studies; it was also a battle over money, jobs, and how much power individuals and departments could wield. On many campuses, African American studies programs were relegated to the status of a poor stepchild, often having the number of full-time positions slashed and receiving less money in their operating budgets than more conventional departments, all of which made it difficult to attract good teachers and competent scholars. Some other programs, such as those at Cornell and Harvard, survived by setting themselves apart from the university and becoming virtually autonomous. Gates was equally critical of this practice, insisting that it "ghettoized" African American studies to the point at which "students and members of the faculty sit around and argue about whether a white person can think a black thought." Instead, Gates envisioned African American studies programs that were fully integrated into the life of a college or university but which, like more conventional departments, maintained the power to make appointments to the faculty. He also hoped that in such programs, and, indeed, because of them, blacks and whites could come together to teach African American studies for all interested students, whatever the color of their skin might be.[4]

TEACHING AT DUKE

Given the persistent effort to persuade Gates to come to Durham, he was stunned by the response his hiring aroused. Because of the money his various publications had earned, Gates could afford certain luxuries out of reach for ordinary college professors. For instance, Gates, Appiah, and Finder all drove expensive automobiles, which some members of the Duke faculty did not appreciate. Gates's purchase of an old and expensive Victorian house also aroused resentment and anger among the Duke community. Others criticized Gates for what they called his "entrepreneurial energy" and the large financial rewards that it afforded him. Many on campus, black and white, accused Gates of having sold out. A flattering profile of Gates published in the *New York Times* as "Black Studies' New Star" did not help to endear him to his new colleagues.[5]

Yet what seemed the most serious affront to many people in Durham was that Gates had married a white woman, something that even in the 1990s many white Southerners found impossible to accept. As Gates commented, "It was pure, unadulterated racism. I had never experienced that kind of thing before." Although Gates was used to hearing racial slurs, to hear them from academics in the college community was devastating for him and his family. When asked in a magazine interview about her family's time in Durham, Sharon Gates stated, "I hate to say it, but some of the black faculty members at Duke . . . just did not make trouble. But Skip was going to make trouble. He was going to be opinionated and loud. He was going to bring people there who were opinionated and loud, and they didn't want it."[6]

2 LIVE CREW CONTROVERSY

In the fall of 1990, Gates further inflamed the controversy swirling about him when he became involved in the obscenity trial of the popular rap group 2 Live Crew. Earlier that summer, United States District Court Judge Jose Gonzalez of Fort Lauderdale, Florida, had declared the album *As Nasty as They Wanna Be* obscene in the three counties under his jurisdiction. Gonzalez's pronouncement was a first; a Federal court had never before deemed a recording obscene. Adding to the controversy, a record-store owner who defied the judge's order and continued to sell the album was arrested. Not long afterward, two members of 2 Live Crew were also arrested for performing their songs before an adults-only audience in Florida. If convicted, they faced hearty fines and a possible prison sentence.[7]

For the trial, the defense attorneys for 2 Live Crew called three expert witnesses to explain the origins and meaning of rap music, arguing that a more complete understanding of the history and culture from which rap emerged would show it to be anything but obscene. The witnesses included John Leland, a music critic for *Newsday*, who was considered an expert on hip-hop and rap, and Gates, who had written about the place of rap music in African American culture. According to one of the lawyers for the group, Gates was to give testimony that would portray 2 Live Crew as "literary geniuses."[8]

In October, Gates flew to Florida to testify. As one journalist described the courtroom encounter, Gates "approached his task as any college professor would on the first day of class. Peering through his spectacles, he lectured about the relationship among art, literature, black culture and the 2 Live Crew." When asked to explain the group's music, Gates stated that "One of the brilliant things about these four songs is they embrace that stereotype [of the black gangsta]. They name it and they explode it. You can have no reaction but to bust out laughing. The fact that they're being sung by four virile young black men is inescapable to the audience. Everyone understands what's going on. Their response is to burst out laughing. To realize it's a joke. A parody." Gates hesitated before continuing: "That's p-a-r-o-d-y."[9]

For Gates, rap music was another form of "signifyin'." As he explained in an interview, "When you're faced with a stereotype, you can disavow it or you can embrace it and exaggerate it to the nth degree. The rappers take the white Western culture's worst fear of black men and make a game out of it." In part based on Gates's testimony at the trial, the group was eventually acquitted of all charges.[10]

If Gates was already on shaky ground at Duke with his peers, his court appearance did little to help matters. Nor did his article in the *New York Times* that defended the group, rap music in general, and the right to freedom of expression. Soon after the trial, conservative professors and the student newspaper targeted him. Even though Gates is an avowed political moderate, he was being vilified for having radical leftist and even Marxist sympathies. To his disappointment, he did not get the support he had expected from the black faculty or from his African American peers at other colleges and universities. Some were openly critical, questioning his actions and his judgment. Houston A. Baker, Jr., himself a renowned literary scholar and a professor of English, wrote that although Gates was "one of the best representations imaginable of the unanticipated emergence of excellence," his defense of 2 Live Crew was "a form of expert witnessing that deflects serious attention from the complexities of popular Afro-American expressive cultural studies" and marked the "drearily conventional mode of response by adult scholars to popular cultural forms."[11]

HARVARD CALLING

Circumstances did not improve for Gates at Duke. When, in 1990, representatives from Harvard contacted Gates about the possibility of coming there to teach, he was more than prepared to listen. On January 31, 1991, the university made Gates a generous offer. He would receive a joint appointment in the departments of English and Afro-American Studies, and the directorship of the W. E. B. Du Bois Institute for Afro-American Research. Gates accepted.

When news of his leaving Duke broke, the criticism came fast and hard. One columnist writing in the *Durham Herald-Sun* declared that Gates did not show "any loyalty beyond the paycheck," adding: "Now Harvard is falling over itself to give Gates the sun, the moon and the stars—the latter especially to his liking—while Duke ends up with pixie dust." Students circulated a David Letterman-style "Top Ten" flier on the campus that listed "money" twice among the chief reasons Gates was leaving Duke for Harvard. An editorial in the student newspaper titled "Skipping away again" accused Gates of having "done almost nothing for the University." Gates's response was straightforward. He voted with his feet, leaving Duke and Durham as quickly as he could.[12]

In an interview he granted to *Time*, Gates was asked about his experience in the South and whether there were still differences with the North with regard to race relations. Gates replied:

> Relations are worse in the South because the bottom-line historical experience was slavery. In the North it was abolition. A black person is not at the same place societally in the North and in the South for that very reason . . . Here I was the first black person to live in my immediate neighborhood. I came home one day and a brick mason, who was black, was redoing the walk. And I said hello. And he said, "Can I help you?" with a bit of hostility in his voice. And I said, "You are helping me. You're fixing my walk." And he looked dumbfounded and said, "Is this your house?" And I said, "Yeah." And he said, "Do the white people know that you bought this house?" I said, "Of course!" And he said, "Of course. I bet they know all about you." And we both busted out laughing, like I'd been checked out. On the whole I'd rather live in the North than in the South.[13]

Harvard had its own motives for luring Gates away from Duke. Gates's appointment represented a last-ditch attempt to save a department that was floundering. Despite its reputation and prestige, Harvard had fared no better than many other academic institutions with its African American studies program. Like other institutions, Harvard's African American studies program was established amid the political protests of the 1960s. But since its creation, the department had struggled to stay rigorous and relevant. Professors criticized the quality of the scholarship coming from the department, characterizing it as mediocre at best. Others believed that the department was in the clutches of black student radicals. Worse, the department believed the administration had consistently overlooked and neglected it in favor of the more established disciplines on campus.[14]

By the beginning of the 1990 academic year, the department appeared ready to collapse and die. At that point, only one tenured professor was affiliated with the department and only a handful of students had declared majors in the field. Adding insult to injury, those students often had to attend classes at nearby Tufts University or

Boston University to meet their requirements. The department and the affiliated Du Bois Institute struggled to attract reputable scholars. In 1991, with considerable pressure from students to remedy the situation, Henry Rosovsky, the former dean of the Faculty of Arts and Sciences and former chair of the economics department, and Harvard president Derek Bok decided to make one final effort to salvage the department. Rosovsky had been following the fortunes of the department since the beginning, having served as the chairman of the committee that established it. By this time, he was skeptical about the chances for survival. He nevertheless gathered a task group to discuss possible solutions. Among those present at these meetings was Peter Gomes, then the acting director of the Du Bois Institute. Gomes recalled the state of affairs:

> Harvard [was] not accustomed to being criticized for inadequacies or craven stupidity. We had tried to make a number of distinguished senior appointments, and none of these people would come because signing on to Afro-American studies at Harvard was like signing on to crew the *Titanic*. It was a big ship, but it was sinking fast. And who wanted to sacrifice their career even for the glory of a Harvard appointment? Names were floated about, and one name that consistently appeared was that of Henry Louis Gates Jr.

For Rosovsky, who along with Bok was preparing to retire, the opportunity to hire Gates was important. As Rosovsky later said, "We didn't want to leave that one last item in poor condition. So we went out to look for the person who could do it, and we got Skip [Gates]."[15]

When first approached, Gates was unsure about the situation at Harvard and whether he wanted to take on the task of repairing it. When offered the job, Gates thought, "the department had been cursed. Afro-American studies here [at Harvard] were about to be shut down." But Rosovsky assured him that Harvard was serious not only about rebuilding the program but also about creating the best African American studies program in the world. Gates was intrigued and also realized that, finally, the ideal situation to build a department on his own terms had arrived. Combined with his unhappiness at Duke, Gates had no question about accepting the job.[16]

BUILDING A DEPARTMENT

Despite his eagerness to get away from Duke and to begin his work of reconstruction at Harvard, Gates and his family had a difficult time making the transition. Gates's wife, Sharon, feared that the new job would take him away from his family for increasingly long periods. His children also had trouble adjusting to the colder climate of Massachusetts and were unhappy at their new school. Sharon missed her friends and had no job. Making things even more depressing, the family discovered that they were not immune from racism even in the North.[17]

These concerns notwithstanding, Gates hit the ground running at Harvard. Before he had even officially joined the faculty, Gates had already started to build a consortium of sorts, meeting with all the department chairs and with the senior black faculty. Telling them that he needed their help and advice, Gates made it clear that he was counting on them to help him build a successful and thriving department. His next move was to secure new office space. He then hired three new professors, including Appiah, with the hope of eventually bringing in even more powerful names in the field.[18]

Gates also suggested joint appointments with other departments on campus, such as the Divinity School, and the music, fine arts, and history departments. In the past, this sort of undertaking had been particularly thorny because of the skepticism on the part of members of other departments about the quality of work being done in the African American studies program. Gates then tried to expand the course offerings, in one instance inviting African American film director Spike Lee to teach a seminar. The course was filled to capacity, with Lee agreeing to come back to teach it again the following semester. All of these moves were also part of Gates's plan eventually to offer graduate degrees in African American studies.[19]

Gates also took some significant, if symbolic, steps to enhance the reputation of African American Studies at Harvard. He dug up photographs of his five predecessors and had them framed and displayed in the department's new offices that overlooked Harvard Square. As Gates told an interviewer "You have to approach the mantle you inherit with a great deal of humility . . . Every other person in this job

Harvard University professor Henry Louis Gates, Jr., left, appears with film director Spike Lee, in 2006, in Edgartown, Massachusetts, prior to the screening of a segment of the four-part documentary film by Lee, When the Levees Broke: A Requiem in Four Acts. *Gates was instrumental in bringing Lee to Harvard in the early 1990s to teach a seminar on Contemporary African American Cinema. (AP Photo/Steven Senne)*

was sharp, I am not of a different order than they. Yet the image of the place has been nothing but failure since 1969." To friends, he commented, "First time I've ever had a real job . . . I've been a free agent. This is the first time I've been in a position to build something outside myself."[20]

Possibly one of the most important decisions Gates made was to secure Henry Rosovsky as a mentor and a confidant. As Gates admitted:

> I knew about raising money for grants, but I didn't know anything about running a department. Rosovsky and I talked about everything. He was like an uncle to me. It was like teaching somebody how to drive a car. Here's a door, open it, get in, here's the steering wheel. I knew nothing about running a department—how to recruit

> people, how to negotiate with the dean, how do you persuade people to come. Rosovsky taught me about Harvard, how people work here. One time after we'd talked, I was walking through Harvard Yard, and I thought, This is like a minefield in Cambodia, and I just left the guy who has the map to where the mines are. There is a way of functioning here, a way you're supposed to be. . . . You can't storm the gates. Just because somebody tells you that there's a hole in your idea that doesn't mean that they're a racist.[21]

Gates also used his position as a consulting editor for Oxford University Press and other publishing houses to reach out to other African American faculty on the campus. He went to all the black academics and told them that he would help with their publishing endeavors. In addition, Gates brought with him two growing legacies: *Transition*, with Henry Finder now the magazine's managing editor, and the Black Periodical Literature Project. Gates also courted, cajoled, and engaged movie stars, entertainers, executives, and media moguls from all throughout the world who, either through donations of money or teaching of classes, would add to the cachet of the department. Gates envisioned a department of black intellectuals that, in addition to boasting great talent, would also have money and power.

It seemed that all of Harvard and a good part of the country were now watching Gates. On campus, many saw Gates as a "black Messiah." The student newspaper, *The Harvard Crimson*, went so far to ask "Can He Save Afro-Am?" Peter Gomes who was on the initial hiring committee had no qualms about Gates "He's the Second Coming . . . Or maybe he's the First Coming. He makes all the difference in the world."[22]

THE DREAM COMES TOGETHER

In a short time at Harvard, Gates established himself as a major player in the field of high-power academic politics. In part, this was so because Harvard's academic environment was such that someone like Gates could build a power base among those eager or desperate to establish and solidify their careers. Harvard already had an established history of academics who had gone on to bigger roles in American society and government, such as the economist John Kenneth Galbraith and the political scientists Daniel Patrick Moynihan and Henry Kissinger. Nor was such success confined to the social sciences. In science, James D. Watson and Walter Gilbert had used research conducted at Harvard to advance the genetics and the biotech industries.[23]

For Gates, coming to Harvard meant the opportunity to rebuild the African American studies department and to show critics and skeptics that the discipline as a whole was alive and well. "Because of Harvard's national pre-eminence, what happens there gives Afro-American studies an intellectual legitimacy for other places," said Cornel West, then the director of the Afro-American studies program at Princeton—a program considered by many at that time to be the best in the country. "What's happening at Harvard makes it more difficult to trash Afro-American studies." Gates's efforts paid handsome dividends. Within one year, the number of Harvard undergraduates majoring in African American studies had almost doubled, going from 19 to 37 students.[24]

Gates first year, though, was not without problems. His attempts at working with other departments and calling for cooperation between white and black faculty members did not sit well with some of the more radical members of the student body. He also disappointed some African American students because he did not share their black nationalism or subscribe to the Afrocentric views that taught, for instance, that the ancient Egyptians had been black and that Western civilization had derived almost wholly from African antecedents.

Gates also riled some with his own critique of African American studies, which he characterized as "intellectually bogus" because, among other faults, they are guilty of inventing an African past that never existed. Additionally, Gates criticized departments that did not take a hard look at the enduring problems African Americans faced, such as racism, poverty, unemployment, drug addiction, crime, and violence and were instead content to debate whether "Cleopatra was black." Yet Gates was adamant. "Those of us serious about Afro-American studies have to establish the field with the greatest integrity," he stated in an interview. "We are presiding over the era of the permanent institutionalization of the field—or its failure. It's crunch time."[25] For Gates, rigorous scholarship rather than "ethnic cheerleading" would, in the end, sustain African American studies.[26]

Despite his attitude toward Afrocentrism and his disagreements with the more radical students, Gates did extend an olive branch, inviting comment about the department and its offerings. In a further effort at conciliation, Gates also agreed to hold an informal reading course that focused on Afrocentric writings.

THE DREAM TEAM OF AFRICAN AMERICAN ACADEMICS

More than anything else, Gates's highest priority was to put together what he called a "dream team" of the greatest black scholars in the world. His vision was to establish the greatest center of intellection concerning persons of African descent in the Old World and the New World.

> What I want to see happen, from a purely academic point of view, is I'd like to see people in our department be part of the generation that ends that cycle that African American studies have been trapped in for a century—each generation has to reinvent the wheel, the basic facts, things as basic as how many slaves left the West Coast of Africa boarded on ships, and how many got off on the other side. Those basic facts have never been established. You kill a field that way. I think we are doomed or blessed to be the generation that finally digs everything up so that another generation can do dazzling, brilliant, elaborate analysis.[27]

At the top of his wish list was Cornel West, a best-selling author of 11 books, a political activist, a theologian, a philosopher, and a commentator on social theory and race relations. At that point, West was a professor of religion and the director of the African American studies program at Princeton. Gates enticed West to come to Harvard in 1995.[28]

Over the next decade, Gates successfully hired other prominent African American scholars. Suzanne Preston Blier, an expert in African art and architecture, joined the program, as did Lawrence D. Bobo, a specialist in race relations, and Evelyn Brooks Higginbotham, whose work was in African American women's history. James Lorand

Matory, a scholar specializing in African and Afro-Latin religions, also joined the department. Staying on was literary historian Werner Sollers, who was the sole professor remaining in the department when Gates came to Harvard. In 1996, a year after taking West from Princeton, Gates hired William Julius Wilson, a well-respected expert on urban poverty, from the University of Chicago. Wilson stated that he came to Harvard because he was intrigued by Gates's desire to build a program similar to that at Chicago. Wilson also was taken by Gates's vision of a department that was expansive and looking from the black experience outward rather than merely focusing on the minutiae of the black experience itself.[29]

One of the criticisms that dogged Gates was the shortage of women on his dream team. "We do not have enough black women," he conceded in one interview. "We've made offers that were turned down. We should have more black women here and I hope that we are able to get them. It ain't for want of trying." Another criticism of Gates's department is it is left leaning in its politics. But Gates has stated that, again, it has not been for lack of trying; he simply has not been able to attract a black conservative or an Afrocentric scholar who would fit into the Harvard faculty.[30]

As he built his department, Gates was also demonstrating his skills at raising money, bringing $8 million in pledges for the department. He has also enhanced the profile and glamour of the department by bringing in as guest lecturers jazz musician and pop music producer Quincy Jones and film director Spike Lee, among others. One of Gates's most significant achievements has been the wooing of noted art collectors Jean and Dominique de Menil to donate their acclaimed photo archive of blacks in western art to the W. E. B. Du Bois Institute.[31]

To some academics, Gates and his dream team, with their celebrity and their appeal to an audience beyond academia, make them and their scholarship suspect. But for the majority, Gates had performed a miracle in a relatively short period of time that boosted Harvard's African American studies department into being a serious academic contender with the likes of Temple University and Princeton. As Harvard's then-president, Neil Rudenstine, declared, "Different institutions have different temperaments and personae, and Harvard's always been a place where outspoken public intellectuals and scholars coexisted, either side by side or often in the same person." Henry Rosovsky had nothing but praise for Gates's initial efforts, stating, "He's had an extraordinary impact on the university. . . . He's raised the level of Afro-American studies in people's eyes at Harvard."[32]

And though some critics believed that Gates was too much in the limelight, it may not have been entirely of his doing. According to Aldon D. Morris, a professor of sociology at Northwestern University, "American society tends to latch on to one black person as the one to pay attention to. . . . In many ways, Skip [Gates] has been selected by the elite establishment to play that role." He's not to be blamed for being treated as if he's the only black academic in the world."[33]

Still some academics believed that Gates was acquiring too much influence. One African American scholar stated, "It's the Booker T. Washington syndrome." Another commented, "To be critical of Henry Louis Gates in public would be like cutting your own throat. Everybody is always going to check with him in terms of tenure, in terms of any kind of grants. He is going to be the one the mainstream turns to for verification that a person of color knows what they're doing." As far as Gates was concerned, the comparison to Washington was moot, commenting, "I reject that comparison. . . . It's a joke for me. When Booker T. was around, only one Negro controlled things. There's nobody like that now. . . . You can't be perceived as being successful in any field in this country without being resented to some extent."[34]

In the years ahead, Gates's scholarship and personality continued to be scrutinized by whites and blacks alike. What had begun as a rumbling in academic quarters grew louder as Gates's star continued to ascend and shine.

NOTES

1. Adam Begley, "Black Studies New Star," *The New York Times*, April 1, 1990, Section 6, 24.

2. Cheryl Bentsen, "Head Negro in Charge," *Boston Magazine*, July 23, 2009, http://www.bostonmagazine.com/articles/Henry_Louis_Gates_Jr/page5.

3. Jack E. White, Sharon E, Epperson, James L. Graff, "The Black Brain Trust," *Time*, February 26, 1996, http://www.time.com/time/magazine/article/0,9171,984176,00.html.

4. Adam Begley, "Black Studies New Star," *The New York Times*, April 1, 1990, Section 6, 24.

5. Ibid.

6. Bentsen, "Head Negro in Charge."

7. Jon Pareles, "An Album is Judged Obscene; Rap: Slick, Violent, Nasty and, Maybe Hopeful," *New York Times*, June 17, 1990, Section 4, 1.

8. Ibid.

9. Ibid.

10. Ibid.

11. Bentsen, "Head Negro in Charge"; David Nicholson, "Race, Culture and Morality," *The Washington Post*, June 13, 1993, X5.

12. Bentsen, "Head Negro in Charge."

13. Breena Clarke and Susan Tifft, "A Race Man Argues for a Broader Curriculum: Henry Louis Gates Jr.," *Time*, April 22, 1991, http://www.time.com/time/magazine/article/0,9171,972763-2,00.html.

14. Fox Butterfield, "Afro-American Studies Get New Life at Harvard," *The New York Times*, June 3, 1992, Section B, 7.

15. Ibid.

16. Ibid.

17. Bentsen, "Head Negro in Charge."

18. Ibid.

19. Ibid.

20. Denise K. Magner, "Nomadic Scholar of Black Studies Puts Harvard in the Spotlight; Henry Louis Gates, Jr., uses clout and flair to lead his department out of mediocrity," *Chronicle of Higher Education*, July 15, 1992, http://chronicle.com.ezproxy2.rmc.edu/article/Nomadic-Scholar-of-Black-St/78462/.

21. Bentsen, "Head Negro in Charge."

22. John Powers, "Henry Louis Gates, Harvard Man," *Boston Globe*, May 12, 1991.

23. Bentsen, "Head Negro in Charge."

24. Butterfield, "Afro-American Studies Get New Life at Harvard."

25. Magner, "Nomadic Scholar of Black Studies Puts Harvard in the Spotlight; Henry Louis Gates, Jr., uses clout and flair to lead his department out of mediocrity."

26. Butterfield, "Afro-American Studies Get New Life at Harvard"; Bentsen, "Head Negro in Charge."

27. Bentsen, "Head Negro in Charge"; Breena Clarke and Susan Tifft, "A Race Man Argues for a Broader Curriculum: Henry Louis Gates Jr.," *Time*, April 22, 1991, http://www.time.com/time/magazine/article/0,9171,972763-2,00.html.

28. Ibid.

29. Ibid.

30. Ibid.

31. Ibid.

32. Ibid.

33. Magner, "Nomadic Scholar of Black Studies Puts Harvard in the Spotlight; Henry Louis Gates, Jr., uses clout and flair to lead his department out of mediocrity."

34. Ibid.

Chapter 9

"ACADEMOSTAR"

Throughout the 1990s, even as Henry Louis Gates, Jr. built a department at Harvard, he continued work on his own scholarship. His many projects included a major collection of writings on the trans-Atlantic slave trade, one of the first books of its kind on the subject. Gates also wrote three books and co-authored two others, one with his colleague and friend, Cornel West. In between there were magazine articles, critical book reviews, and op-ed pieces for such publications as *The New Yorker, The New York Times, Time, Sports Illustrated,* and *The National Review.* Gates even took on and conquered another medium: television.

Gates's relationship with *The New Yorker*, in particular, was proving to be very lucrative professionally and financially. Not only was he a noted scholar, he was also becoming a recognized journalist, even making it to the finals of the National Magazine Awards, which is the magazine industry's equivalent of the Pulitzer Prize. Helping him, too, was the arrival in 1994 of Henry Finder, the former editor of *Transitions*, at *The New Yorker.* Because of his writing for *The New Yorker*, Gates was emerging not only as the country's most celebrated African American intellectual and scholar, he was also, in effect, assuming the role of the "chief interpreter of the black experience" for white America, a role that did not always sit well with other African American leaders.[1]

LOOSE CANONS (1992)

In 1992, Gates published *Loose Canons: Notes on the Culture Wars*, a collection of previously published essays that dealt with various aspects of multiculturalism. The controversial subject was charged with emotion. The phrase *culture wars* referred to the broad-based conflict over differing values among various political, ethnic, and religious groups. Debates raged between conservatives and liberals about such issues as homosexuality, abortion, women's rights, gun control, censorship, race, affirmative action, and the separation of church and state. The term *culture war* first surfaced in the United States during the 1960s, but it was not until the 1991 publication of James Davison Hunter's book *Culture Wars: The Struggle to Define America* that the term became more firmly embedded in American public discourse. A professor of sociology at the University of Virginia, Hunter described the dramatic transformation that had taken place in American political and cultural life: the emergence of polarizing divisions that made reasoned discourse and productive compromise almost impossible. In Hunter's analysis, two warring groups had come to dominate the debate on every controversial issue, their views shaped by increasingly rigid ideologies. Nowhere was this battle for the heart and mind of the United States being fought with greater tenacity than on college campuses.

The title of Gates's book refers to out-of-control individuals who can sabotage and endanger, whether intentionally or unintentionally, the cohesion and purpose of a group. In this case, the "loose canons" are those who make honest dialogue about differences of opinion and values so difficult. In the 10 essays that comprise the volume, Gates tried to steer the middle course through the culture wars. It was no easy task. For Gates, the key to healing the divisions that threatened to sunder the United States into permanently warring ideological camps lay in reforming American education. He scolded conservatives for their insistence that Western civilization was a "universal culture" when, in point of historical fact, the culture itself had been driven by a series of contradictions and conflicts. Gates also criticized Afrocentrists and other radicals who viewed the West as evil and attributed a kind of purity to the cultures of the so-called developing world.

Gates focused on education because he believes that a curriculum reflects prevailing attitudes and values. What the young are taught reveals what a society regards as truth and what values it holds most dear. The culture wars had made agreement on such basic matters more difficult, if not impossible, to attain. Although Gates argued that African American studies should not be forever condemned to occupy an academic ghetto, he had no wish to abandon the traditional curriculum. Rather, he proposed that it be broadened, for example, to include the narratives of the slaves next to the plays of Shakespeare. Ultimately, Gates sought to encourage discourse and understanding rather than to acquiesce in the present dissent and division, which he knew could only deepen mistrust, anger, and hatred.[2]

Gates writes, "Ours is a late-twentieth-century world profoundly fissured by nationality, ethnicity, race, class, and gender. And the only way to transcend those divisions—to forge, for once, a civic culture that respects both differences and commonalities—is through education that seeks to comprehend the diversity of human culture." For Gates, the challenge to American universities is simple but not easy: to live up to the standards they espouse. The great challenge, as Gates sees it, will be to shape a common culture that in its responsive to difference, whether of color, class, religion, sexuality, or gender embraces rather than vilifies them.[3]

COLORED PEOPLE (1994)

In the summer of 1992, Gates was attending a Rockefeller Foundation Conference in Bellagio, Italy, near Lake Como. One morning, he was so struck by the beauty of the lake and its surroundings that it reminded him of his hometown of Piedmont, West Virginia, which was located near the Potomac River. Gates began composing letters to his two daughters, sometimes writing as much as 20 or 30 pages a day. During the next four weeks, Gates lost 10 pounds but had the rough draft for what became his next book, the autobiographical *Colored People: A Memoir*, which was published in 1994.

Colored People was Gates's recounting of his childhood, adolescence, and young adulthood in Piedmont between the 1950s and the early 1970s. Gates wrote the book with several purposes in mind. One was to deal with the grief he felt at his mother's death and to offer a tribute to his parents for all they had done to raise and nurture him. In an interview, Gates described how, watching his daughters grow up, he came to appreciate the things that his mother and father had done that, at the time, had frustrated and angered him. Gates also tried to recapture the era by retelling his father's stories. Gates later said the most satisfying response to his book came from his brother Rocky who told him, "You got Daddy's voice."[4]

Gates also believed it was very important for his daughters to know what life was like for black people in a segregated world. Gates related a story that illustrated the point:

> [We were] riding along on Route 2, which connects Cambridge with Lexington, Massachusetts, and it was 1991, it was on Martin Luther King's birthday, and they were hearing for the 10,000th time "I have a dream" on the radio. And so Maggie said, you know, "Daddy, what was the civil rights movement all about?" And I said, "Well, you see that motel?" And she said, "Yeah." And I said, "I couldn't have stayed in that motel 30 years ago." I said, "Your mama could have stayed at that motel, but your mama couldn't have stayed at that motel with me. And I looked in the rearview mirror and she was nudging Liza like, "God, you know, here's another lie." I mean, they couldn't believe that this could be true.[5]

Gates thought it important to discuss the racism of the period not in abstract but in personal, human terms by relating specific instances such as his not being able to eat at the Cut-Rate, having to attend separate churches, and not being able to date white girls. Told against the backdrop of the emerging civil rights movement, *Colored People* is at once a memoir and history lesson about the fight against segregation and with a heavy price paid for victory, not least the loss of an intimate black world and way of life.

The publication of *Colored People* brought Gates even more fame, moving him further beyond the confines of academia. The book was widely praised for its humor and insight into the nature of race relations at a pivotal moment in American history. But not everyone was enamored with Gates's account. One reviewer stated that Gates "may have nostalgic feelings for that lost world, but his 'personal destiny' was to leave it far behind him and to find his place in its polar opposite, the world of scholarship. . . . If the book seems informal, even folksy, it is because Gates has worked to make it that way, reaching down from his ivory tower in an effort to recapture a black West Virginian patois with which, in fact, he is quite clearly uncomfortable."[6]

THE FUTURE OF THE RACE (1995)

Taking as his inspiration and point of departure W. E. B. Du Bois's essay "The Talented Tenth," published in 1903, Gates produced *The Future of the Race* in collaboration with colleague Cornel West. Published in 1995, the book, as the title suggests, focuses on the future of black people in the United States. The 1990s proved rich and fulfilling for many educated and affluent African Americans. In sharp contrast, conditions were deteriorating for the black middle class and poor. Combining memoir and biography with social and cultural analysis, Gates and West examined the reasons for and proposed solutions to rectify this state of affairs. The Talented Tenth to which Du Bois had referred in the original essay was that exceptional group of African American men and women who had reached great heights and would lead the black community out of poverty and despair. These were individuals who used their education and talents to serve their people without succumbing to selfishness and greed. By 1948, Du Bois had revised his earlier assessment of the Talented Tenth, for he had often found them wanting. His belief that higher education would foster generosity and goodwill had foundered; instead, education had produced men and women who were, by turns, egotistical, selfish, and self-serving, focused only on their personal advancement at the expense of the very people they were supposed to help. Du Bois never gave up hope, but certainly tempered his enthusiasm and expectations.

For Gates, the racial progress that Du Bois had envisioned would occur only with the rise of a new kind of political leadership, one that de-emphasized the idea of race. In other words, he thought that for African Americans to move forward required that the emphasis on the creation of a separate black community must be lessened. West, by contrast, believes that being African American is inherently tragic, that Du Bois's ideal of the Talented Tenth will never be fully realized, and that black Americans will continue to struggle for a long time to come.

THE NORTON ANTHOLOGY (1996)

Moving away from the distressing state of the African American community, Gates followed *The Future of the Race* with the much-anticipated *Norton Anthology of African-American Literature*, the culmination of 10 years of hard work come to fruition. The "Nortons," as this series of anthologies is often called, are among the most widely used college texts for the study of literature. Since the publication of the *Norton Anthology of English Literature* in 1961, the series has sold 15 million copies. Although there have been other anthologies of African American writing, the Norton publication was different. The addition of a Norton text on black literature meant the recognition of a formal canon of written texts that is acknowledged as great literature worthy of serious study. As Gates stated in an interview, "There is no more question of the legitimacy of this literature." Working with Gates on the book was Nellie McKay, a professor of Afro-American literature at the University of Wisconsin.[7]

An introductory essay summarized each entry in the volume; there was also biographical information and footnotes. Included in the 2,665 pages bound in a single, two-and-a-half-pound volume was the first known short story written by an African American, "Le Mulatre" ("The Mulatto"), by Victor Sejour. The work was located in the Bibliotheque Nationale in Paris; its appearance in the Norton Anthology marked the first time the story had been published in English. Also included was the poetry of Phillis Wheatley, a slave brought to America from Senegal who became the first African American to publish a book in English. In addition, there was a wide selection of works from authors such as Toni Morrison, Langston Hughes, and James Baldwin, as well as rap, gospel, and jazz lyrics and sermons, poems, and slave narratives. Also included with the written text was a CD-ROM that contained speeches by the Rev. Dr. Martin Luther King, Jr. and Malcolm X, jazz by Duke Ellington and Louis Armstrong, and a rendition of "Rosie" by inmates of a prison farm. There were also sections of the book that focused on African American literature during Reconstruction (1865–1877), the Harlem Renaissance (1920s), and the late-twentieth-century Black Arts Movement. Of the 120 entries in the anthology, women write 52.

When Gates first thought of the anthology, he was not sure that such a book would sell the necessary 5,000 copies needed for the press to break even. Gates need not have worried; the initial printing of 30,000 copies sold out so rapidly that Norton issued a second run of 20,000 additional copies. The success of the book, according to Gates, was in part due to the growing presence of African American literature in mainstream America. "There used to be one black writer now and then on the best-seller list," he noted in an interview. "Now there are sometimes three or four black authors at the same time. Black Americans bought 160 million books last year."[8]

LIVING LARGE

By the spring of 1996, Gates's fame had reached new heights. In April, *The New Yorker* published its "Black in America" issue, for which Gates served as the guest editor. To publicize the issue, the magazine held a party at Harvard. Two of the articles that Gates had commissioned did not please everyone; one was a profile of William Julius Wilson, who had just come to the department, and the other was a profile of stock trader Alphonse "Buddy" Fletcher, who had just endowed a $3 million professorship at the W. E. B. Du Bois Institute. Some believed that it was both self-serving and a conflict of interest on Gates's part to have included the articles.[9]

That same year, Gates moved his family into an $890,000 residence located on Francis Avenue in Cambridge, known as the Writer's Block or Smart Street to local residents. The neighborhood was home to a number of celebrated writers and personalities, including chef Julia

In 1998, Henry Louis Gates, Jr., was presented the National Medal of Arts and the National Humanities Medal. Gates is pictured here with former president Bill Clinton during the awards ceremony, on November 5, 1998, at the White House. (AP Photo/Doug Mills)

Child and the economist John Kenneth Galbraith. By this time, Gates's wife, Sharon, had established a landscape design business and his two daughters were enrolled in upscale private schools. The family enjoyed summer vacations on Martha's Vineyard, long a popular spot for the rich and famous, and in the Caribbean. Gates was estimated to be earning as much as a million dollars a year, a stratospheric salary for most people, let alone for a college professor. He had come a long way from his humble origins in Piedmont, West Virginia.[10]

For many people, the life that Gates led was now more in keeping with that of a celebrity than a retiring scholar. When traveling overseas, Gates took the *Concorde* and stayed at the most exclusive hotels. He hobnobbed with movie stars, directors, and politicians, taking great delight in his celebrity status and the benefits that accompanied it. Many of Gates's colleagues found his behavior embarrassing, with one voicing his exasperation with Gates's "endless and irritating childlike wonder."[11]

THIRTEEN WAYS OF LOOKING AT A BLACK MAN (1998)

"This is a book of stories," wrote Gates, "and all might be described as 'narratives of ascent.'" So began the preface to the collection of essays *Thirteen Ways of Looking at a Black Man*, published in 1998, in which Gates interviewed a number of high-profile black men, including writers James Baldwin and Anatole Broyard, former General and Secretary of State Colin Powell, religious activist and politician Jesse Jackson, actors Harry Belafonte and Sidney Poitier, and Nation of Islam leader Louis Farrakhan. Despite the common thread of rising above poor or modest origins, Gates hoped to show that the "unitary black man" is as imaginary as the creature that poet Wallace Stevens wrote about in his poem "Thirteen Ways of Looking at a Blackbird." Gates also demonstrated how each man's character and personal experiences, as well as race and class, helped shape him and his perceptions of the world.[12]

With these essays, Gates hoped to make readers feel as if they were eavesdropping on conversations among blacks. A central theme of each profile is the way in which the men struggled with the challenge of being representatives of their race while at the same time being true to themselves. As with many of his writings, in *Thirteen Ways*, Gates maintains the hope that current and future generations of African Americans will feel "free enough to reveal how we really feel to white people."[13]

By 1997, Gates's many accomplishments earned him recognition as one of the "25 most influential Americans" by *Time*. The magazine described him as displaying a combination of "the braininess of the legendary black scholar W. E. B. Du Bois and the chutzpah of P. T. Barnum. The chairman of Harvard's Afro-American-studies department has emerged as a prolific author, a whirlwind academic impresario and the de facto leader of a movement to transform black studies from a politically correct, academic backwater into a respected discipline on campuses across the U.S."[14]

ENCARTA AFRICANA (1999)

The end of the 1990s brought one of Gates's most ambitious undertakings to fruition: the Afropedia project. The Afropedia emerged from humble beginnings in 1973 when Gates, Kwame Appiah, and Wole Soyinka met at an Indian restaurant in London for dinner. After a few bottles of wine, the three pledged to put together a pan-African encyclopedia.[15]

For Gates, the dream of such an endeavor was again born out of the influence of W. E. B. Du Bois, who first conceived of the idea in 1909 after the publication of the *Encyclopedia Judaica*, a reference work dealing with the history of the Jewish people. "Du Bois thought in 1909 that the principle cause of racism was ignorance," said Gates during an interview, "And if he could marshal scientific evidence—that was his phrase—what then? We could defeat racism. And the best way to marshal scientific evidence was through an encyclopedia." Initially, Du Bois wanted to focus on the history of black peoples throughout the world but faced sharp criticism from within the African American community. The project was never completed.[16]

Gates, Appiah, and Soyinka also wanted their encyclopedia to be inclusive. As Gates stated, "You have a diasporic black world, and the only way to put it back together again is symbolic. It's like Humpty Dumpty. Whoever could edit the Encyclopedia Africana would provide symbolic order to the fragments created over the past 500 years. That is a major contribution."[17]

In 1979, Gates, then an assistant professor at Yale University, approached *Encyclopedia Britannica* with the idea of producing an encyclopedia modeled on Du Bois's vision. But the company could not be convinced that the project would make money. Representatives told Gates that if he could raise the funds needed to cover the cost of publication, they would produce the encyclopedia. In 1995, Gates decided to try again. This time, backed by promises of development monies from Quincy Jones, the popular composer and record producer, and Martin Payson, a high-ranking executive at Time Warner, Gates went to Random House. The company was intrigued by the project and asked Gates to consider making a CD-ROM of the encyclopedia. Gates then went to Dynamic Diagrams, a Rhode Island design group that produced a CD-ROM prototype of the encyclopedia. But when Gates returned to Random House with it, he was told that the company was no longer interested. "They said that they were only doing games," Gates recalled, "I could have cried. I was devastated."[18]

In 1997, Gates and Appiah teamed up again with Quincy Jones and Martin Payson to start Afropedia, an independent company that would produce an *Encarta Africana.* The work was to be modeled on the popular Microsoft encyclopedia Encarta. It was the group's hope that the *Encarta Africana* would become the high-tech version of W. E. B. Du Bois's dream, an encyclopedia of the black world on CD-ROM.[19]

By this time, joint business ventures between educational institutions, scholars, private donors, and corporations were becoming more common. Knowing that they would need a great deal of money to succeed, Gates and his partners looked for some kind of corporate partnership. It was a hard road; many mainstream publishers were not interested. Finally, the group managed to interest Microsoft, the inventor of the Encarta Encyclopedia, to devote $1 million to the project, as well as to provide technical, design, and production support. Another million dollars came from Perseus, a publisher, which would subsequently produce a printed version of the encyclopedia. In addition, Gates negotiated a reported $100,000 consulting fee for the project and financial equity for himself for both the online and publishing versions of the *Encarta Africana.*[20]

On a logistical level, bringing *Africana* to fruition took 15 months filled with complications, disappointments, and bitterness. There were punishing deadlines to be met in order to create a massive reference work that ran to an estimated 2.25 million words. Plagiarism was rampant. Despite the publication being about black people, there were few black writers on the staff. The tiny budget (at least by modern publishing standards) also made it hard to complete the project.

In addition, the very nature of the project was such that both sides (Microsoft and Gates and his partners) were unsure of what to expect.

Microsoft had never undertaken a joint venture of this type before; responsible for supervising the project, Gates and his partners in Afropedia had the final say about contents. Also unlike most encyclopedias, Encarta encyclopedias are completed at a pace unheard of in traditional publishing, moving from start to finish in little more than a year.[21]

Then there was the model to adopt and follow. Writers of encyclopedias have three models from which to choose: the *Samuel Johnson Dictionary*, in which one person writes the entire work; the *Encyclopedia of Islam*, in which only experts in a chosen field write the entries; or the *Encyclopedia of Social Sciences*, which relies on a core staff to write the work. In the case of *Africana*, two models were melded together in

Chairman of the Afro-American Studies Department at Harvard University, Professor Henry Louis Gates, Jr., left, stands with fellow members of the Africana.com Web site editorial board, including Professor K. Anthony Appiah, center, and Dr. Harry M. Lasker III, on the steps of Widener Library on the Harvard campus in Cambridge, Massachusetts, on Monday, January 31, 2000. Africana.com is an educational portal that accompanied publication of the 2,095-page book Africana, *billed as the first international encyclopedia of black history and culture. (AP Photo/Christopher Pfuhl)*

which a core crew of writers were responsible for writing approximately 40 percent of the book and a group of experts the remaining 60 percent. To attract writers, the Africana website posted ads around Cambridge offering 15 cents a word. Those who applied and were hired were mostly undergraduate and graduate students, though some professors also contributed entries.[22]

WORK BEGINS

Problems arose almost immediately. Since the project was being done privately instead of under the aegis of Harvard University, some writers did not have access to the campus libraries and instead had to go to the small African American studies center at Barker Center or make use of the *Encyclopedia of African-American Culture and History*, which had been edited by contributor Cornel West, or the online reference resource Lexis-Nexis. When the first entries began coming in, the editors were appalled at the poor quality of the writing; there was also a problem with plagiarism. More staff had to be hired to rewrite the plagiarized sections of the encyclopedia. By this time, Gates was off campus filming a television project and was not available to maintain some sense of quality control. As one staff member later admitted, "There were huge, huge mistakes that never would have eluded Skip [Gates] had he seen them." Adding to the already tense situation were the rapid deadlines that made editing the entries, especially those of inferior or dubious quality, a nightmare for the project editors.[23]

Other concerns surfaced over how few African American writers were working on the project. Some argued that had the company spent more money on writers' pay, they might have attracted better, or at least more reliable, talent, including experienced black writers. Also problematic was that none of the core editing staff were African American. Many associated with the project found it puzzling that so few blacks wanted to work on the encyclopedia, especially given Gates's high profile and reputation.[24]

Despite the many problems associated with producing the encyclopedia, the introduction of the *Encarta Africana* was hugely successful. Taking a cue from its Encarta predecessors, the encyclopedia featured more than 3,300 entries, live videos, virtual tours, and other innovative features. The encyclopedia drew strong praise from many in the academic community. "The sheer magnitude of its size, scope and chronology—from four million BC to the present—is magnificent in itself," said Dr. Robert L. Douglas, professor of art history and pan-African studies at the University of Louisville in Kentucky. He continued, "Only with the coming years of its use in the multitude of educational forums and the research potential that it promises for teachers and scholars will its successes and failures be realized." Gates was also pleased with the way the project turned out, declaring, "I'm really proud of this product. I would do it the same way over again."[25]

But not everyone was as happy with the outcome as was Gates. Dr. Raymond Winbush, a professor at Fisk University, Du Bois's undergraduate alma mater, took sharp exception to what he believes is the underrepresentation of Afrocentrics, that is, those members of the black community who believe that Africa should be the focus of all African American study. "It's like a modern history of computing without mentioning Bill Gates," he said in one interview. Molefi Kete Asante, a widely published author and former chairman of the African studies department at Temple University in Philadelphia, agreed: "What we have here is a commercial product for the white buyers . . . It is a project that is flawed, because the people who created it, even though they have strong credentials in the white academies, do not understand the African world."[26]

Ever the conciliator, Gates agreed that *Encarta Africana* was "mainstream, very mainstream." But he also argued that it should in no way lessen the importance of the encyclopedia or diminish the quality of the scholarship. Gates also noted that the scholars involved in the project worked hard to include opposing viewpoints on and interpretations of black history and culture. "We don't have a God complex," Gates stated. "We are not saying that this is the Bible." But what perhaps confirmed Gates's sense of accomplishment was the letter he received from David G. Du Bois, the 71-year-old son of W. E. B. Du Bois, which stated in part that he and Anthony Appiah, "inspired by Father's original idea, have made a magnificent, state-of-the-art contribution to African and African American studies and humanities with Encarta Africana. Dr. Du Bois would have been proud."[27]

CONQUERING A NEW MEDIUM

Beginning in 1996, Gates set out in another new direction when he and his family were filmed for a segment of the BBC Television series *Great Railway Journeys*. A series of travel documentaries, each episode focuses on a well-known figure traveling by train to a country in which he or she has a personal connection. For Gates's episode, the journey was from Great Zimbabwe to Kilimatinde, the area to which he had traveled decades earlier while a student at Yale. He was accompanied on the 3,000-mile trip through Zimbabwe, Zambia, and Tanzania by his wife and two daughters. The trip ended at Kilimatinde, the small city where, 25 years earlier, Gates had worked in the hospital.

Although filled with thoughtful reflection and emotion, the episode also provided unexpected moments of humor and irony. As one television critic summed it up, "a sermonising father determined to broaden his children's minds is trailed by two reluctant (and sharp-eyed) teenagers, counting the days until they can get back to the mall." The critic also noted that any attempts on Gates's part to engage the locals on the evils of colonialism fell flat, as one Zimbabwean stated how he longed for the return of white rule, while some Zambian women protested their lesser status due to prevailing tribal traditions. But it was Gates's daughters who stole the show from their father. At times complaining, at others sarcastic, the two clearly resisted the idea that their heritage began in the hot, dusty, and often impoverished places they visited. When Gates and his wife Sharon were "adopted" by a Ugandan tribe, one of their daughters, speaking directly into the camera, said: "I thought it was so funny when he [the chief] told my mother 'These are your people,' because they're not . . . They're not even my people."[28]

Gates had better luck a few years later launching the PBS series *Wonders of the African World*. For Gates, working on the series was another opportunity of a lifetime. The program allowed him to challenge the widely held Western view of Africa as the dark and primitive continent that became "civilized" only with the arrival of the white man. In an interview for the PBS website, he stated:

> From the time I was a little kid I had a fantasy of doing a TV series called the *Wonders of the African World* that would be equivalent of the 7 wonders of the world. I don't think that people know very

> much at all about Africa. If they think about Africa quite frankly what comes to mind? Poverty and flies, famine, war, disease and maybe some big game. How many people know anything at all about the truly great ancient civilizations of Africa, which in their day were just as glorious and just as splendid as any on the face of the earth.[29]

The six-part series took Gates from Egypt to the Sudan, and then down the Swahili coast of East Africa and through portions of West Africa. In doing the series, Gates hoped to bring into American homes and classrooms the history of the African peoples who created great civilizations, had rich cultures, possessed vast knowledge, and built proud cities. He also hoped to share on some level his personal journey as an African American, the great-great-grandchild of slaves now returning to the area known as the Slave Coast. As Gates reiterated in another interview: "It's important to debunk the myths of Africa being this benighted continent civilized only when white people arrived. In fact, Africans had been creators of culture for thousands of years before. These were very intelligent, subtle and sophisticated people, with organized societies and great art."[30]

The series was filmed in 12 countries over a period of one year. Gates traveled by small plane, boat, and jeep to his destinations. The result was a visually stunning presentation that offered viewers the sights and sounds of Africa that many had never before seen or imagined. There were several high points to Gates's travels, such as the discovery of nearly 50,000 ancient volumes written by black men in Arabic and Gates's memorable visit to Nubia. He later confided that "To be able to go there, and to be able to film the pyramids where 40 generations of black pharaohs and black queens are buried, was quite amazing for me." Another high point was a visit to the church that Ethiopians believe holds the Ark of the Covenant, which is guarded by a single man whose entire life is devoted to the cause.[31]

Certainly one of the most poignant moments of the series was the visit to the Door of No Return, which is part of the House of Slaves museum and memorial to the Atlantic Slave Trade, located on tiny Goree Island off the coast of Dakar, Senegal. The spot is said to memorialize the final exit point of enslaved Africans bound for the New

World. Although scholars disagree about how many African slaves were actually held and then transported from the island, the large numbers of visitors, including African Americans and important heads of state from countries the world over, testify to the immense human tragedy that took place along the Slave Coast. For Gates, who had visited the site before, this visit was extremely emotional:

> I cried in the slave castle when I was alone. I mean I just cried. One, I cried for my ancestors who obviously made it. Two, I cried for the pain and anxiety of being wrenched away from your family and all that was familiar . . . It would be like dropping, like a hole opening up in this floor and dropping out. And then the brutality in the middle passage, on the plantations in the New World. Would I have made it? I don't know if I could have made it . . . But somebody in my family made it. So I must have the genetic material to survive, otherwise we wouldn't be having this conversation.[32]

Yet, for all the adventure and poignancy the series brought to the screen, there were moments when Gates seemed to struggle with his expectations and the realities he witnessed. Gazing at the Aswan monuments, for instance, he noted the "blackness" of the pharaohs. During the 1960s, the monuments were submerged under water to create the Aswan Dam. Gates asked whether the monuments were targeted because of the "blackness" of their occupants and wondered whether they had not been victims of Arab racism. While visiting residents of Kenya and Zanzibar, Gates was taken aback when they informed him that they are not African but are instead of Arab or Persian descent. Gates replied that "To me, [these] people look about as Persian as Mike Tyson." Gates also seemed to be searching for accountability for the slave trade on the part of African peoples.[33]

Again, like many of the undertakings with which Gates has been involved, controversy erupted over *Wonders of the African World*. Although many mainstream publications, such as the *New York Times* and *The Christian Science Monitor*, praised the series, many others, notably black and Afrocentric publications and websites, soundly condemned the series and Gates. Many took Gates to task for his commentary.

Afrocentrist professor Molefi Kete Asante commented that "If Gates were a white traveler in Africa . . . the NAACP and a host of human rights leaders . . . would have considered his production an insult and an assault on African people. However, because he is black we must call it a travesty." The African historian Joseph Inikori complained that "Even as a travelogue, one would expect Professor Gates' commentaries to be better informed as a scholar, even if not as an Africanist."

Some Afrocentrists also accused Gates of "sowing the seeds" of discord between African Americans and the peoples of the African continent by trying to repair race relations between black and white Americans through shifting the main burden of "guilt" over slavery from whites to Africans. Critics believed that this approach was too simplistic, and Gates was overlooking the complexity of African participation in the slave trade. One critic put the argument forcefully: "The message I get is: I'm Professor Gates and my saying [it] makes it so and the hell with your scholarship. I'm black, a professor and it's Africa, right? And PBS, BBC, the Guggenheim Museum et al. agree with me." It would be precisely these types of criticisms that continued to dog Gates well into the next decade.[34]

NOTES

1. Cheryl Bentsen, "Head Negro in Charge," *Boston Magazine*, July 23, 2009, http://www.bostonmagazine.com/articles/Henry_Louis_Gates_Jr/page7.

2. Philip Burnham, "Culturally, Gates Holds His Middle Ground," *The Washington Times*, May 17, 1992, B7.

3. Mark Edmundson, "Literature in Living Color," *The Washington Post*, June 7, 1992, Book WoWorld, X6.

4. "Booknotes: Colored People by Henry Louis Gates, Jr.," October 9, 1994, http://www.booknotes.org/Watch/60633-1/Henry+Louis+Gates.aspx.

5. Ibid.

6. Jonathan Yardley, "Back Where He Started From," *The Washington Post*, May 15, 1994, Book World, X3.

7. Dinitia Smith, "Centuries of Writing by Blacks Distilled into a Single Volume," *The New York Times*, December 12, 1996, Section C, 15.

8. Ibid.

9. Bentsen, "Head Negro in Charge."

10. Ibid.

11. Ibid.

12. Henry Louis Gates, *Thirteen Ways of Looking at a Black Man* (New York: Random House, 1997), xi–xxvii,

13. Ibid.

14. "Henry Louis Gates," *Time Magazine*, April 21, 1997, http://www.time.com/time/magazine/article/0,9171,986206-4,00.html.

15. Craig Offman, "The Making of Henry Louis Gates, CEO," *Salon*, June 16, 1999, http://www.salon.com/books/it/1999/06/16/gates.

16. Michel Marriott, "Planet Africa: Black History on Disk; Henry Louis Gates Jr. and Microsoft Produce a Long-Awaited, Much-Debated Encyclopedia," *The New York Times*, January 21, 1999, Section G; Page 1.

17. Offman, "The Making of Henry Louis Gates, CEO."

18. Marriott, "Planet Africa: Black History on Disk; Henry Louis Gates Jr. and Microsoft Produce a Long-Awaited, Much-Debated Encyclopedia."

19. Offman, "The Making of Henry Louis Gates, CEO."

20. Bentsen, "Head Negro in Charge"; Offman, "The Making of Henry Louis Gates, CEO."

21. Offman, "The Making of Henry Louis Gates, CEO."

22. Ibid.

23. Ibid.

24. Ibid.

25. Marriott, "Planet Africa: Black History on Disk; Henry Louis Gates Jr. and Microsoft Produce a Long-Awaited, Much-Debated Encyclopedia"; Offman, "The Making of Henry Louis Gates, CEO."

26. Marriott, "Planet Africa: Black History on Disk; Henry Louis Gates Jr. and Microsoft Produce a Long-Awaited, Much-Debated Encyclopedia"; Offman, "The Making of Henry Louis Gates, CEO."

27. Marriott, "Planet Africa: Black History on Disk; Henry Louis Gates Jr. and Microsoft Produce a Long-Awaited, Much-Debated Encyclopedia."

28. Thomas Sutcliffe, "Review," *The Independent* (London), September 19, 1996, 32.

29. Henry Louis Gates, "Interview," http://www.pbs.org/wonders/fr_bh.htm.

30. Ibid.

31. Gloria Goodale, "Seeing the 'Wonders of Africa' through Fresh Eyes," *Christian Science Monitor*, October 22, 1999.

32. Gates, "Interview."

33. Hishaam D. Aidi, "Slavery, Genocide and the Politics of Outrage: Understanding the New Racial Olympics," *Middle East Report*, n.d., 1.

34. Molefi Kete Asante, "Whose Africa Is It Anyway, Or, What Exactly Is Skip Gates Signifyin'?, *African Arts* 33, no. 2 (Summer 2000): 3–5.

Chapter 10

"YOU CAN'T DO EVERYTHING"

The beginning of a new decade—and a new century—saw Henry Louis Gates, Jr. busier than ever. But amid continuing successes with the publication of several works by African American authors, appearing on several television programs, and increasing public exposure through magazines and newspapers, Gates was also dealing with a number of issues, including the break-up of his "dream team" department of African American studies at Harvard. He was also the subject of headlines when a local policeman mistakenly arrested him for breaking into his own house.

Controversy also continued to dog Gates through the decade over his increasing influence and media exposure. Still, despite the criticisms, Gates continued to move forward with his own work. Among his many projects was the quest to learn more about his own family background as well as that of others; in the process, he learned some interesting facts about his heritage. Gates also continued to speak out in support of a multicultural curriculum while maintaining a centrist position in politics and the ongoing cultural wars.

TROUBLE AT YALE

The year 2000 was barely underway when Gates was again caught up in a controversy, this time at his alma mater, Yale University. At a February ceremony held to honor Gates, the president of Yale, Richard C. Levin, when describing Gates's many accomplishments with the field of black studies and of the African American studies department at Harvard, told the audience, "We have watched with interest and admiration, and a little jealousy." Among the people in the audience was the current head of the Yale African American studies department, Hazel V. Carby. Carby took offense at Levin's remarks and shortly after offered her letter of resignation to the university. In her letter, Carby told university officials that Levin's comments had tarnished her program's reputation, writing, "To be jealous of [Harvard's] department is to invite a comparison that can only be interpreted to mean that we do not reach a standard of which you can be proud." Carby also asked that if the president wanted an equivalent program to that at Harvard, why did he not support Yale's African American studies program with more adequate resources and monies?[1]

Carby's resignation set off a chain of events that threatened to unravel relations between the administration, faculty, and students. President Levin sent a letter to the faculty and graduate student body apologizing for his remarks and stating that he did not intend to embarrass or insult Carby.

But that was not the end of the incident. According to the student paper, the *Daily News*, other faculty members had approached Carby, telling her that Gates had boasted that Levin had approached him, asking him what it would take for Gates to leave Harvard and come to Yale to helm its African American studies program.[2]

When news of the debacle reached Gates, he was by all accounts genuinely surprised at the fracas. He later told the educational newspaper *The Chronicle of Higher Education* of his tremendous respect for Carby and that he never had any intention of leaving Harvard to come to Yale. Then suddenly, six days after the incident made the news, Ms. Carby decided to stay on in the department. It was believed that her decision was made in light of an earlier meeting of Yale's governing board, who had decided to seriously consider offering the African

American studies program, which was spread among several departments, its own departmental status in the near future. However, some Yale professors were not completely satisfied with the outcome. Robert Stepto (who won tenure instead of Gates in the English department in 1973) believed that Gates had spread the rumors about his coming to Yale himself, in part because of his refusal for tenure many years earlier. As Stepto told the *Daily News*, "I strongly feel that Skip Gates is a provocateur and even a saboteur." However, when pressed to explain his remarks further, Stepto declined.[3]

BONDSWOMAN'S NARRATIVE (2002)

In 2001, Gates underwent hip-replacement surgery. During his convalescence, he stayed at home, where he happened to come across a catalogue for a sale of African Americana at a New York gallery. Gates was still an avid collector of African American literature, and he scanned the contents of the catalogue to see what was listed. Among the documents and ephemera, there was one item that immediately caught his interest: lot 30—an unpublished manuscript titled *The Bondwoman's Narrative by Hannah Crafts, a Fugitive Slave, recently Escaped from North Carolina.* According to the catalogue, the manuscript was the autobiography of a slave woman who had escaped from her master.[4]

Gates realized that the manuscript was one of three things: a fake; or the manuscript was of the period but the writer was not an African American; or it was an authentic work of African American literature. He decided to take a chance and contacted a friend to buy it on his behalf. Gates later said in an interview, "I thought it would auction off at tens of thousands of dollars . . . it was good that I didn't appear at the auction because I feel the level of interest would have increased thereby driving up the price." In the end, the manuscript cost Gates $8,500; in return, he received a bundle of 300 yellowing and extremely fragile pages that showed much scribbling. But once again, his instincts paid off: *The Bondwoman's Narrative* proved to be an authentic fictionalized slave narrative that would eventually be published in book form.[5]

As it turned out, *The Bondwoman's Narrative* appears to be the earliest novel ever written by an African American woman, making the work not only a great literary discovery but also an important historical document. According to Professor Nellie McKay, who worked with Gates to authenticate the manuscript, "My feeling was, here's one more piece of evidence that not only were there African-Americans who could read and write, but African-Americans who had some sense of how to put narrative together to make a story." What made the narrative even more special was that it still was in handwritten form rather than printed. As Gates explained in an interview, "This is the first glimpse we have had of the pre-edited, unmediated consciousness of a slave. This is major."[6]

The Bondwoman's Narrative makes for fascinating reading. The story begins on a plantation called Milton, located somewhere in Virginia. Hannah Crafts works as a house slave for the Vincent family. When Mrs. Vincent is revealed to have a slave mother, she and Hannah flee Milton. Unfortunately, Hannah is caught and sold again, this time to the wealthy Wheeler family in Washington, D.C. The family eventually moves to North Carolina. As Hannah writes of her new mistress, "I never felt so poor, so weak, so utterly subjected to the authority of another, as when that woman with her soft voice and suavity of manner, yet withal so stern and inflexible, told me that I was hers body and soul, and that she did and would exact obedience in all cases and under all circumstances."[7]

The Wheeler family proves to be difficult and hard to work for; they have already lost two slaves as runaways, and it is clear they are not about to let that happen a third time. But when Hannah learns that her mistress is going to make her marry a field slave against her will, Hannah decides she must escape. She succeeds in getting away from the Wheelers and takes a ship to New Jersey and to her freedom. Crafts eventually marries a minister and creates a school for black children.

The book is riveting, not only for the story but also for the remarkable and harrowing picture it paints of the life of an enslaved black woman. Crafts's descriptions of being looked over by two slave owners, who debate her qualities as if she is a piece of meat, is chilling. Her vulnerability and inability to control her life, even to whom she can marry, is heartbreaking. But her resolve and courage to escape to a better life also point to an individual who, despite her bondage, maintains her dignity in the face of crushing indignities suffered on a daily basis.

After acquiring the manuscript, the next step for Gates was to prove beyond a doubt that the manuscript was authentic. To establish that the actual manuscript was a product of the period, he went to an expert in historical documents, who established that the ink used to write the text consisted of iron gallotannate, a mixture of oak gallnuts, iron sulfate, and gum; these ingredients were widely used in the mid-nineteenth century to make ink. Crafts used a goose quill to write her story; the expert was also able to prove that the paper she wrote on was of the period as well. The handwriting of the manuscript was also of interest; the writing is looping and at times appears uncertain. According to one expert, this suggested that the writer was learning to write as she wrote her story. As Professor McKay stated in an interview, "This woman seems to have had . . . a broad knowledge of the literature of the time . . . She obviously didn't know how to use that very well . . . but she had that information, and in a certain way knew how to use it." For Gates, then, it appeared that what he had purchased was the working copy of Crafts's manuscript written in her own hand.[8]

In addition, Gates made a list of all the proper names in the book in an attempt to authenticate as many as possible of the people and places that Crafts wrote about. He proved successful in his search of historical records, in which he found a slave owner by the name of Wheeler who lived in North Carolina. The records also noted that Wheeler had been involved in a dispute with one of his runaway slaves by the name of Jane Johnston. Crafts, in her book, described how one of the runaway slaves of the Wheeler family had been called Jane.[9]

Professors of literature and American studies have been quick to point out that whether or not Hannah Crafts actually existed, *The Bondwoman's Narrative* would still stand as an important contribution to American and African American literature. Gates was determined to find out who Hannah Crafts was, but so far, has been unable to track her down. After the publication of *The Bondwoman's Narrative*, Gates donated the manuscript to Yale University; at that point, the manuscript was estimated to be worth $350,000 dollars.[10]

THE DREAM TEAM BREAKS UP

With the departure of President Neil Rudenstine from Harvard in 2001, Gates and his department became embroiled in a number of events that threatened to tarnish the reputation of the African American studies department and his dream team. Taking Rudenstine's place was Lawrence H. Summers, who at first glance did not seem to be as wholly committed to the African American studies program as well as to racial diversity. The department, which was enjoying the fruits of Gates's formidable fund-raising activities (the department reportedly had a $40 million endowment), would soon be fraught with tension and conflict.

The relationship between President Summers and Gates's department got off to a shaky start. Summers failed to make an obligatory courtesy call to the department after he arrived, even though he had paid his respects to other academic departments. Unlike his predecessor, Neil Rudenstine, who had wholeheartedly supported Gates and his department, Summers's attitude toward black studies was indifferent at best. Summers also remained tightlipped about the college's commitment to affirmative action. It would be after repeated requests from the liberal newspaper the *Boston Globe* that Summers actually made a statement, which was considered to be lukewarm at best, about affirmative action at Harvard. The president also hinted that Gates and the black studies department would no longer be considered a top priority item by the college.[11]

Cornel West, in particular, was becoming a figure of increasing controversy, in part because of his advising two other highly controversial figures: Nation of Islam's leader Louis Farrakhan, with the Million Man March in 1995, and New York political activist Reverend Al Sharpton, who was mounting a possible presidential run for 2004. West had also made a rap CD and was lecturing to inmates at prisons.[12]

In October 2001, President Summers reportedly told West to curb his outside activities as well as criticizing West for grade inflation, a problem not confined to the black studies department. Summers also hinted that some of West's activities such as his recording of a rap CD, as well as his writing of newspaper and magazine articles, did not constitute serious scholarship, despite the fact that West ranked higher in academic citations than the majority of professors on the campus. West, believing that he had been insulted by Summers, questioned publicly Summers's commitment to the African American studies program and to the policy of equal opportunity. The uproar led to West, Kwame Appiah, and even Gates threatening to leave Harvard for Princeton with its high-powered African American studies program.

Even the Reverend Al Sharpton became involved when he threatened to sue Summers for interfering with West's activities. The Reverend Jesse Jackson also condemned Summers and demanded the "unequivocal commitment to affirmative action (at) our flagship university."[13]

In taking the controversy outside of Harvard's walls, West apparently hoped to stir up press attention that would portray the Harvard dream team in a favorable light. At one point, national talk show host Tom Joyner told his listeners (who numbered around 30 million) to call Summers in defense of West and Gates. However, not all was as it seemed. In an article for *The Village Voice*, writer Thulani Davis pointed out that it was in Joyner's best interests to stir up the controversy because of an earlier business deal he had with Gates and the fast-food giant McDonald's to sell black history booklets with the purchase of a meal. Joyner was also involved with Gates in a deal with Scholastic Press to publish a teacher's curriculum guide to be distributed by Coca-Cola.[14]

In January 2002, Appiah took Princeton up on its offer and resigned. Despite overtures from Summers, Cornel West also left for Princeton in April. That left Gates, and for several months, Harvard anxiously waited for the other shoe to drop. As Jesse Jackson commented, if Gates left Harvard, his defection would quite simply "blow a hole in the fuselage of academia."

Gates remained largely silent on the departures of Appiah and West, only lamenting the breakup of his once powerful dream team. In the end, Gates decided to stay, reaffirming the belief that Summers was committed to the continued success of the department. But that did not stop other members of the African American studies department from leaving Harvard. In 2005, the husband-and-wife academic team of Lawrence D. Bobo and Marcyliena Morgan left the department to take jobs at Stanford because Summers refused to tenure Morgan. After Summers left Harvard, the two returned to Harvard in 2007 to continue their teaching.[15]

The drama surrounding the eventual departure of West and Appiah stirred up long-simmering resentments among academics, black and white. As Davis pointed out in her article, although Gates and West had many supporters who condemned Summers's actions against West as belittling and demeaning, others saw the episode as possibly leading to a backlash against other academics in African American studies throughout the country. Just as the discipline was regaining a stronger foothold, due in part to the efforts of Gates at Harvard, the kind of fallout precipitated by the struggle at Harvard "when privileged men call the race troops to arms for no greater reason than to enhance their already cushy careers," does not help other academics. Or, as one anonymous Ivy League professor angrily commented, "It is tawdry to be called upon to go to bat in what is really a negotiation for further job advantage, when people are out of work, millions are going without health care, and there are real problems."[16]

A SCHOLAR AND ENTREPRENEUR

By 2002, Henry Louis Gates appeared to be a one-man business. His colleague and friend Wole Soyinka described Gates as that rare combination of intellect and industry, with a finger in many literary and media pies. Not only was he the author of eight books, but he was also associated with the publication of 119 additional titles, in 164 editions, spread among 48 different publishing houses and imprints. Thirty-two of the titles listing his name were books in which he wrote forewords or introductions. In addition, 71 titles listed Gates as either an editor or co-editor. Also, Gates had a contract to provide six articles a year for the *New Yorker* magazine as well as writing essays, op-ed pieces, reviews, and other articles for a number of other newspapers and periodicals. By all accounts, it was an astounding publishing record for a scholar.[17]

While some of these publications were the result of arrangements Gates made with some of his publishers, the astounding number of publications that bear his name is also testimony to the power Gates wielded as head of the African American studies program at Harvard and his successful career. In addition, according to one anonymous source in publishing, Gates also receives royalties from books that he contributes to, which is an unusual occurrence in the publishing world. In addition to this are monies that Gates earns from his online endeavors such as *Encarta Africana.*[18]

Besides his lucrative publishing and multimedia ventures, Gates also earns impressive amounts for speaking engagements. At one point, Gates and Cornel West were earning between $15,000 and $20,000 when they spoke as a team for university visits. Speaking alone, Gates earns well in the range of $10,000 or more. These sums on top of his publishing, plus Gates's salary at Harvard, put him well within the seven-figure range, if not more. As expected, Gates's earnings are also a source of complaint among other scholars. However, as Caryl Phillips, professor of English at Columbia University in New York, stated in his defense, Gates "took the path of scholarship, then chose to become a major player, a kingmaker; it's essentially a political role," which has earned him not only a higher profile than that of most scholars but an especially lucrative position as well.[19]

AFRICAN AMERICAN NATIONAL BIOGRAPHY (2005)

By 2004, Gates had steadied his department, and it appeared both he and Harvard had weathered the storm with Summers. After the departure of Appiah and West, Gates made several impressive hires that bolstered the reputation of the department. He also undertook another new project, this time working with another member of the black studies team, Evelyn Brooks Higginbotham, in assembling the first volume of a projected 10-volume series to be called the *African American National Biography*.

Even as the *The African American National Biography* was underway, Gates and Oxford University Press published *African American Lives*, in April 2005, which drew on the biographical information being compiled for the *National Biography* project. Gates called *African American Lives*, a 1,050-page book, the "all-time greatest hits" of African American history. The volume contained the biographies of 611 African Americans, spanning more than four centuries. The volume includes, among others, the story of Esteban, the first African known to have set foot in North America, and Onesimus, the former slave of Boston minister Cotton Mather, who is credited with introducing the process of inoculation during the 1721 smallpox epidemic. The volume also includes the life stories of a number of teachers, artists, writers, political activists, and athletes. Meanwhile, Gates continued his work on the *The African American National Biography*, which would contain over 4,000 biographies of notable African Americans. At the same time, an ongoing online resource to the set was also created, bringing the total number of biographies to more than 5,000 entries. It stands as the largest African American biographical research project to date.

In an interview about the project, Gates stated, "You can't restore what has been truly lost. You have to find it first, preserve it and then put it in the mainstream." Once again, Gates in his role of historical and literary archaeologist successfully reversed "centuries of neglect" by putting together such a massive reference work. In addition, Gates secured funds to have the reference work put in the public school libraries in the cities of Boston, New Orleans, Seattle, and Washington, D.C. Eventually, Gates hoped to have additional copies given to other school libraries throughout the country.[20]

One of Gates's big concerns was that African American children learn that black role models are not just athletes and rap musicians but encompass every field and discipline. "Sooner or later, we hope that we'll be able to create a new range of role models other than hip-hop stars and people living the gangster life and embracing the bling-bling," Gates remarked. Many in the education field applauded Gates's efforts. Allen Smith, a professor at Simmons College's Graduate School of Library Science, stated that many reference works have overlooked the contributions of black Americans, making it difficult to do serious research in African American history. Gates's encyclopedia is a step in the right direction, Smith remarked, "Every generation should produce its own reference works. . . . This generation is, and that's good."[21]

AFRICAN AMERICAN LIVES (2006)

Gates's next project evolved as the result of a late-night brainstorm. Gates had always been fascinated with and even a little envious of people who knew their ancestry. Despite the fact that his own family tree had been relatively well documented, there were still many questions about his family background that he would have liked to answer. It's reported that after collecting stamps and coins, the next biggest hobby in the United States is genealogy, or tracing one's ancestry. For many Americans, that means looking back through records and finding names. For many African Americans, the names and the records just are not there, and the search for one's roots becomes much more complicated. Then one night, Gates got the idea to pick eight well-known black Americans and then trace their family trees back deep into slavery. When the family could no longer be documented by paper, Gates proposed to do DNA analysis: Y chromosome analysis for the males and mitochondrial DNA for all of his guests and Gates himself.

In 2006, Gates put together and produced the four-part program to be televised on PBS in February. Called *African American Lives*, the program was the first documentary series to employ genealogy and genetic science to provide an understanding of African American history. The celebrities chosen for the program included African American comedian Whoopi Goldberg, musician and producer Quincy Jones, sociologist Sara Lawrence-Lightfoot, neurosurgeon Dr. Ben Carson, talk show host Oprah Winfrey, astronaut Mae Jemison, actor Chris Tucker, and minister and businessman T. D. Jakes. A portion of the program showed each individual having the inside of his or her cheeks swabbed for DNA analysis. During the course of the program, they learned the results of their heritage tests.[22]

Gates was very excited about the program. In a PBS interview, he said, "This is one of the most exciting projects in which I have been involved. . . . No television series has explored black roots both in America and in Africa and used DNA research to investigate the origins of individual African-Americans." Gates also believed that the program would serve as a good introduction for African Americans on how to explore their family histories.

Gates himself learned some surprising news about his ancestry. One of the long-standing stories told to him about his family was that the white ancestor believed to have fathered Jane Gates's children was a man by the name of Samuel Brady. According to the DNA test done, Gates learned that not only was he not related to Samuel Brady but he also had as much European blood as African. In addition, a separate genealogical analysis done for Gates suggested that one of his ancestors was probably an Irish servant, while another was most likely an Ashkenazi Jew. Gates also learned that he is descended from an Irish king, known as Niall of the Nine Hostages, who lived in Ireland around 500 AD. For Gates, it was an amazing discovery. Gates would later learn that his great-great-great-great-grandfather, a free Negro by the name of John Redman, fought in the American Revolution. Gates and his brother were later inducted into the SAR, the Sons of the American Revolution, an organization whose members can directly trace their ancestors to those men and women who fought for American independence.[23]

Gates also learned some other interesting things about African American ancestry. In a talk he gave in 2010, he described that if all African American males were tested for their genetic backgrounds, approximately 35 percent would trace their ancestry to Europe, not Africa. What this meant is approximately 35 percent of all African American males are descended from a white man who most likely impregnated a black female slave. Gates also disputed the widely held notion that many African Americans share Native American blood. In reality, only 5 percent of the African American population has approximately 12.5 percent Native American ancestry.[24]

The program was so successful that Gates followed up in 2009 with *African American Lives—Part II*. The series also became the basis for two best-selling books, *Finding Oprah's Roots: Finding Your Own*, published in 2007, and *In Search of Our Roots: How 19 Extraordinary African Americans Reclaimed Their Past*, published in 2009. In 2010, Gates followed up with another television series, *Faces of America*. This time, Gates traced the ancestry of a number of different people who represented a veritable mosaic of race, including the actors Eva Longoria and Meryl Streep, the writers Louise Erdrich and Malcolm Gladwell, the musician Yo-Yo Ma, the poet and scholar Elizabeth Alexander, and comedian Stephen Colbert.

In November 2007, Gates, working with the Inkwell Foundation and Family Tree DNA, established www.africandna.com the first company dedicated to offering both genetic testing and genealogical tracing services for African Americans. The company is the only one of its kind that provides African Americans with family tree research in addition to DNA testing.[25]

ARRESTED

On July 16, 2009, the unthinkable happened. Gates, who had just returned to Cambridge from an overseas trip to China, could not open the front door of his house. Instead, he entered through the back, but found that he still could not get the door open. He then noticed that the lock was damaged. Gates returned to the front and, with the help of his driver, forced the door open. Because Harvard owns the residence, Gates then reported the problem to the university's maintenance department.

In this file photo taken by a neighbor, on July 16, 2009, Henry Louis Gates, Jr., center, the director of Harvard University's W.E.B. Du Bois Institute for African and African American Research, is arrested at his home in Cambridge, Massachusetts. Gates was accused of disorderly conduct but the charges were later dropped. (AP Photo/Christopher Pfuhl)

At some point, a 911 call was placed to the Cambridge police department by a neighbor, Lucia Whalen. Whalen reported that two black men with backpacks were trying to force their way into the house. Sergeant James Crowley, accompanied by two other officers, arrived at the Gates residence. Crowley went to the front door and knocked. Gates came to the door, at which point Crowley told Gates he was there to investigate a report of a break-in. He then asked Gates to step outside, at which point Gates responded, "Why, because I'm a black man in America?"[26]

In the police report filed by Crowley, the officer states that he believed that Gates lived there, though he did ask Gates for a photo identification to prove that he was in fact a resident of the house. Gates refused at first but then did show Crowley his Harvard identification card. Gates then asked Crowley several times for his identification. At that point, Crowley told Gates he was leaving the house; if

Gates wished to continue the matter, Crowley would speak to him outside. Gates then replied, "Ya, I'll speak with your mama outside."[27]

At that point, Gates stepped on his front porch and continued to yell at Crowley, accusing him of racial profiling and saying that Crowley had not heard the last from him. Crowley then warned Gates that he was becoming disorderly; Gates ignored Crowley and continued to shout, at which point Crowley issued a second warning. When Gates ignored that, Crowley then placed Gates under arrest. Gates was then taken to the police station, where he was booked; four hours later, he was released.[28]

CONFLICTING ACCOUNTS

Gates relayed a slightly different account of the episode four days later on the website for *The Root*, an online magazine for which he serves as editor-in-chief. According to Gates, he first saw Crowley at the door as he was speaking to the Harvard Real Estate Office to make arrangements to have the front door fixed. At Crowley's request, Gates opened the front door, at which point Crowley asked him to step outside. Gates did not immediately obey, instead asking Crowley why he was there. When Crowley told him that he was there because of a 911 call about a possible burglary, Gates replied that this was his house. Crowley then asked Gates for proof of residence, at which point Gates turned to go to the kitchen where he had left his wallet. Crowley followed him into the house; Gates handed the policeman his Harvard University ID card.[29]

Gates then asked Crowley for his name and badge number, but Crowley did not respond to Gates's request. Gates continued to ask, but Crowley had left the kitchen. Gates then followed the officer to the front door. When Gates stepped out onto the porch, he asked the other officers for Crowley's name and badge number. Crowley then turned to Gates and said, "Thank you for accommodating my earlier request," and then placed Gates under arrest.[30]

In a follow-up interview published in *The Root* on July 21, Gates stated that when Crowley asked him to step outside, Gates knew that "the way he said it, I knew he wasn't canvassing for the police benevolent association. All the hairs stood up on the back of my neck, and

I realized that I was in danger. And I said to him no, out of instinct. I said, 'No, I will not.'" Gates also stated that Crowley would not have made the demand had Gates been a white man. Gates also said that the reports of his tumultuous behavior were a "joke," that he was suffering from a severe bronchial infection and was incapable of yelling. Gates also denied making any remarks about the mother of the arresting officer.[31]

FIRESTORM

The arrest of Henry Louis Gates sparked a firestorm across the country. Even as it seemed that the United States was turning a corner in its racial history with the recent election of Barack Obama as the country's first African American president, the ugly specter of racial profiling, racist policemen, and racial injustice loomed overhead. In the days that followed, it seemed as if everyone from students in the Harvard yard to the president himself had something to say about the incident.

What made matters even murkier were the accounts about the arresting officer. According to Crowley's supporters, the police officer was chosen by the African American police commissioner to serve as instructor for a Lowell Police Academy course titled Racial Profiling, a course Crowley had been teaching since 2004. Early in his career, Crowley worked as a campus police officer at Brandeis University. In 1993, Crowley tried to revive Boston Celtics star Reggie Lewis, a black man, with mouth-to-mouth resuscitation after Lewis suffered what would be a fatal heart attack during a game. Among his many supporters were a number of African American police officers who stated that Crowley was a good and fair police officer. Some black officers also stated they would have done the same thing as Crowley in his position.[32]

In the end, the charges against Gates were dropped. The city of Cambridge and its police department issued a statement calling the event an unfortunate one and saying that it should not reflect whatsoever on the reputation and character of Gates. However, Crowley stated that he would not apologize for his actions. The police department also supported Crowley, stating that the officer had simply followed procedure.

During a July 22 news conference, President Obama was asked for his opinion of the incident and how it reflected upon race relations in the United States. Obama replied that he could not comment specifically on the role race played but that he did think that the Cambridge police acted "stupidly." His remarks ignited a number of protests from the law enforcement community, who charged that the president's comments hurt police–community relations and could be seen as a setback to what progress the two parties have made over the years. Even opinion polls showed that the public was angry at Obama's comments, with 41 percent disapproving of Obama's "handling of the situation." On July 24, Obama apologized for his comments, stating that both parties probably overreacted to the situation.[33]

THE BEER SUMMIT

In an attempt to quell the emotions swirling around the arrest of Gates, President Obama called both men and invited them to the White House to discuss the situation over beers. Both men accepted, after which Gates wrote to the *Boston Globe* that "My entire academic career has been based on improving race relations, not exacerbating them. I am hopeful that my experience will lead to greater sensitivity to issues of racial profiling in the criminal justice system."

On July 31, the two men, accompanied by their families, arrived at the White House. Each family was given a private tour, but they came face to face in the library. As Gates recalled in a phone interview, "Nobody knew what to do," he said, "so I walked over, stuck up my hand and said, 'It's a pleasure to meet you.' That broke the awkwardness." The two men also agreed to meet for lunch at River Gods, a popular Cambridge pub, in the near future. They then met the president and joined him and Vice-President Joseph Biden for beers in the White House Rose Garden. The president drank a Bud Light, Crowley had a Blue Moon, and Biden, who does not drink, had a Buckler, which is a nonalcoholic beer. Instead of his usual Red Stripe beer, Gates drank a Sam Adams in honor of his ancestor who fought in the American Revolution. Gates also presented Crowley with his 1994 book, *Colored People*, in which he had inscribed, "Linked together forever in history." In an interview after his visit, Sergeant Crowley said, "What you had today was two gentlemen

In this July 30, 2009, file photo, President Barack Obama, right, and Vice President Joe Biden, left, have a beer with Harvard scholar Henry Louis Gates, Jr., second from left, and Cambridge, Massachusetts, police Sergeant James Crowley in the Rose Garden of the White House in Washington, DC. Gates and Crowley have remained on friendly terms since the "Beer Summit." (AP Photo/Alex Brandon, File)

who agreed to disagree on a particular issue. We didn't spend too much time dwelling on the past, and we decided to look forward."[34]

During an appearance on the *Oprah Winfrey Show* in 2010, Gates told Winfrey and her audience that he and Crowley have remained on friendly terms. Gates also related how he had asked Crowley for a DNA sample. As it turned out, Gates and Crowley are actually distant cousins in that the two share a common Irish ancestor. Gates also received from Crowley the handcuffs used on him when he was arrested. Gates told the audience that he plans to donate the cuffs to the Smithsonian's National Museum of African American History and Culture.[35]

WHAT LIES AHEAD

Henry Louis Gates, Jr. has been called many things: a literary con man, a brilliant politician, an overrated academic, and an autocrat. His critics think of him as an elitist who, even in spite of his 2009 arrest, remains unconnected to the grassroots black community. His role as head of the Black Studies department at Harvard has led one critic to describe Gates as "the emcee at the Cotton Club on the Charles." Further, the department provides "Just enough sepia . . . Professor Gates gives them Kenny G. blackness served up in a brilliant literary format—and that's it."[36]

It is, in part, because of Gates's high visibility that he will continue to act as a lightning rod for both the black and white communities. It is clear that into the first decade of the twenty-first century, Henry Louis Gates, Jr. continues to serve as the most eloquent and passionate voice that describes the black experience to white Americans. If anything, as the criticisms grow louder, Gates has done an admirable job of addressing them when he feels it necessary to do so. As he stated in one television interview, "My whole life is a commitment to the black community. That's the truth—and that's what I respond. My work is in African American studies. Who else is that for if not primarily the black community?"[37]

In spite of his critics, there seems little in the way of stopping Gates as he continues on his journey through African American history and culture. This voyage is all the more remarkable because of Gates's insistence that both blacks and whites can benefit from his discoveries, whether a long-forgotten text, the championing of DNA testing to understand a person's ancestry, or promoting African American studies as a viable, vibrant, and legitimate course of scholarly study.

Certainly part of Gates's appeal is that he is appealing. His writings, compared to those of other scholars, are written for a broad audience. While he takes his role of the leading black intellectual with a grain of salt, he also recognizes the power that this identity brings and is willing to use it to advance his beliefs and work. His writing is a good deal more readable than the works of many of his colleagues. Gates is not just documenting and writing about the black experience in America, he is writing about the American experience and, truly, the history of America is one of a melting pot. It should also not come as a surprise that because of Gates, the interest in the field of African American studies has increased dramatically.

While his critics decry Gates as being more closely aligned in spirit with Booker T. Washington, Gates and his admirers tend to see him as an embodiment of W. E. B. Du Bois. Perhaps he is utilizing the best of what both those men had to offer to the black community. While advocating the importance of Du Bois's "Talented Tenth" and the roles of African American intellectuals, Gates has also incorporated Washington's approach of advancement within white society, not by political struggle but by economic self-advancement, as seen with his forays with the *Africana* CD project, the various encyclopedia and reference works, and his aggressive marketing of himself.

For Gates, his life and achievements are predicated on simple and basic truths. As he stated in an interview:

> You have to do what you have talents to do. For me, it is being an academic. I'm not going to be carrying signs. And I'm not going to be a politician. And I'm not going to be this, that, and the other thing. I have to do what I have to do . . . there are many ways you can serve the black community, and you don't have to be teaching literacy out on the street to be serving the black community. Those people who think the only way you can make a viable contribution to the black community is to work in the ghetto 24 hours a day—they're just shortsighted. The battle's got many fronts, and we need people fighting on all these fronts or else we ain't gonna make it. . . . The thing is, you can't do everything.

With Henry Louis Gates, Jr., however, that will always be the challenge.[38]

NOTES

1. Courtney Leatherman, "Perceived Slight May Produce a Gain for Yale's African-American Studies Program." *Chronicle of Higher Education* 46.25 (2000): A18. Expanded Academic ASAP. Web. October 7, 2010.
2. Ibid.
3. Ibid.
4. Esther Addley and Oliver Burkeman, "G2: Women: A slave woman writes: Last year an American professor stumbled upon a book written by a female slave in the 1850s. Could it possibly be authentic? If so, it would be the earliest known novel by a black woman." *The Guardian* (London), April 4, 2002, G2, 8.

5. Herb Boyd, "Skip Gates 'Discovers' Another Literary Masterpiece," *New York Amsterdam News* 93, no. 16 (April 18, 2002): 16; Addley and Burkeman, "G2: Women: A slave woman writes: Last year an American professor stumbled upon a book written by a female slave in the 1850s. Could it possibly be authentic? If so, it would be the earliest known novel by a black woman."

6. Addley and Burkeman, "G2: Women: A slave woman writes: Last year an American professor stumbled upon a book written by a female slave in the 1850s. Could it possibly be authentic? If so, it would be the earliest known novel by a black woman."

7. Hannah Crafts, *The Bondwoman's Narrative*, edited by Henry Louis Gates, Jr. (New York: Warner Books, 2002), 155.

8. Addley and Burkeman, "G2: Women: A slave woman writes: Last year an American professor stumbled upon a book written by a female slave in the 1850s. Could it possibly be authentic? If so, it would be the earliest known novel by a black woman."

9. Ibid.

10. Ibid.

11. "Is the Magic Gone from Black Studies at Harvard?" *The Journal of Blacks in Higher Education* (Autumn 2004): 91.

12. Maya Jaggi, "Henry the First," *The Guardian*, Saturday 6 July 2002, http://www.guardian.co.uk/books/2002/jul/06/internationaleducationnews.highereducation.

13. Ibid.

14. Thulani Davis, "Spinning Race at Harvard: The Business Behind the Gates-West Power Play," *The Village Voice*, January 15, 2002, http://www.villagevoice.com/2002-01-15/news/spinning-race-at-harvard/.

15. Jaggi, "Henry the First."

16. Davis, "Spinning Race at Harvard: The Business Behind the Gates-West Power Play."

17. Ibid.

18. Ibid.

19. Davis, "Spinning Race at Harvard: The Business Behind the Gates-West Power Play"; Bentsen, "Head Negro in Charge," *Boston Magazine*, July 23, 2009, http://www.bostonmagazine.com/articles/Henry_Louis_Gates_Jr/page6.

20. "Black Biography Project Opens the Pages of History." *Black Issues in Higher Education* 21.9 (2004): 19. Expanded Academic ASAP. Web. October 7, 2010.

21. Ibid.

22. Robin Wilson, "Family Revision." *The Chronicle of Higher Education* 52.26 (2006). Expanded Academic ASAP. Web. October 7, 2010.

23. Ibid.

24. Henry Louis Gates, Jr., "Who's Your (Irish) Daddy?: On St. Patrick's Day, Henry Louis Gates Jr. reflects on an unknown Irish ancestor," *Roots*, March 17, 2010, http://www.theroot.com/views/whos-your-irish-daddy?page=0,0.

25. "Harvard Professor Henry Louis Gates, Jr., Joins Forces with Family Tree DNA to Launch AFRICANDNA.com," AfricanDNA.com, November 17, 2007, http://www.africandna.com/News.aspx.

26. "Cambridge Police Incident Report # 9005127." The Cambridge Police Department, http://www.thebostonchannel.com/download/2009/0720/20120754.pdf.

27. Ibid.

28. Ibid.

29. Charles Ogletree, "Lawyer's Statement on the Arrest of Henry Louis Gates Jr.," *The Root*, July 20, 2009, http://www.theroot.com/views/lawyers-statement-arrest-henry-louis-gates-jr.

30. Ibid.

31. Ogletree, "Lawyer's Statement on the Arrest of Henry Louis Gates Jr."; Maureen Dowd, "Bite Your Tongue," *The New York Times*, July 25, 2009, http://www.nytimes.com/2009/07/26/opinion/26dowd.html.

32. Bill Meyer, "White Cop Who Arrested Black Scholar Henry Louis Gates Taught Class on Racial Profiling to Police," *Cleveland Plain Dealer*, July 23, 2009, http://www.cleveland.com/nation/index.ssf/2009/07/white_cop_who_arrested_black_s.html; Laurel J. Sweet, Marie Szaniszlo, Laura Crimaldi, Jessica Van Sack, and Joe Dwinell, "Officer in Henry Gates Flap Tried to Save Reggie Lewis," *Boston Herald*, July 23, 2009, http://www.bostonherald.com/news/regional/view/20090722cop_who_arrested_henry_gates_im_not_apologizing/srvc=home&position=0.

33. Stuart Taylor, "Sotomayor, Gates and Race," *National Journal* (2009). Expanded Academic ASAP. Web. October 7, 2010.

34. Abby Goodnough, "Gates Reflects on Beers at the White House," *New York Times*, July 31, 2009, http://thecaucus.blogs.nytimes.com/2009/07/31/gates-reflects-on-beers-at-the-white-house/?hp.

35. "The Importance of Ancestry," *The Oprah Winfrey Show*. Television Broadcast. ABC, Chicago, March 9, 2010.

36. Bentsen, "Head Negro in Charge."

37. Ibid.

38. Ibid.

SELECTED BIBLIOGRAPHY

Alexander, Elizabeth. "Pursuing the Pages of History: Yale's Henry Louis Gates and the Roots of Black Literature." *Washington Post* 106 (August 10, 1983), B1.

"An American Culture." *National Review* 43, no. 9 (May 27, 1991), 18.

Begley, Adam. "Black Studies' New Star." *New York Times Magazine* 139 (April 1, 1990), 24.

Bentsen, Cheryl. "Head Negro in Charge." *Boston Magazine*, July 23, 2009, http://www.bostonmagazine.com/articles/Henry_Louis_Gates_Jr.

Bernstein, Richard. "African Oriented: Reviving a Magazine of Change and Ideas." *New York Times* 140 (May 14, 1991), B1 (N), C13(L).

"Booknotes: Colored People by Henry Louis Gates, Jr.," October 9, 1994, http://www.booknotes.org/Watch/60633-1/Henry+Louis+Gates.aspx.

Boyd, Herb. "Skip Gates 'discovers' another literary masterpiece." *New York Amsterdam News* 93, no. 16 (April 18, 2002), 16.

Burnham, Philip. "Culturally, Gates Holds His Middle Ground." *The Washington Times* (May 17, 1992), B7.

Butterfield, Fox. "Afro-American Studies Get New Life at Harvard." *New York Times* 141 (June 3, 1992), B9(N), B7(L).

"Cambridge Police Incident Report # 9005127." The Cambridge Police Department, http://www.thebostonchannel.com/download/2009/0720/20120754.pdf.

Clarke, Breena, and Susan Tifft. "A 'Race Man' Argues for a Broader Curriculum: Henry Louis Gates Jr. Wants W. E. B. Dubois, Wole Soyinka and Phillis Wheatley on the Nation's Reading Lists, As Well As Western Classics like Milton and Shakespeare." *Time* 137, no. 16 (April 22, 1991), 16.

Clary, Mike. "Professor Calls 2 Live Crew 'Refreshing.'" *Los Angeles Times* 109 (October 20, 1990), A20.

Davis, Thulani. "Spinning Race at Harvard: The Business behind the Gates-West Power Play." *The Village Voice*, January 15, 2002, http://www.villagevoice.com/2002-01-15/news/spinning-race-at-harvard.

"'Do the Right Thing': Issues and Images." *New York Times* 138, sec. 2 (July 9, 1989), H1(N), H1(L).

Edmundson, Mark. "Literature in Living Color." *The Washington Post*, June 7, 1992, Book WoWorld, X6.

Gardner, Marilyn. "The Classroom versus the Field of Dreams." *Christian Science Monitor* 83, no. 186 (August 20, 1991), 14.

Gergen, David R. "Harvard's 'Talented Tenth': Harvard's Dream Team of African-American Scholars Could Deepen Understanding of Racial Issues in Our Nations." *U.S. News & World Report* 120, no. 11 (March 18, 1996), 116.

Goodman, Walter. "Frontline: The Two Nations of Black America." *New York Times* 147 (February 10, 1998), B3(N), E8(L).

Goodnough, Abby. "Gates Reflects on Beers at the White House." *New York Times* (July 31, 2009), http://thecaucus.blogs.nytimes.com/2009/07/31/gates-Reflects-on-Beers-at-the-white-house/?hp.

"Harvard Hires a Specialist in African-American Studies." *New York Times* 140 (February 1, 1991), A14(L).

Hentoff, Nat. "Campus Quicksand: Finally, an Attack on Black Antisemitism by a Nationally Prestigious Black." *Washington Post* 115 (August 11, 1992), A17.

Holmstrom, David. "A Vision of a New Racial Tapestry: Harvard Scholar Gates Talks about Racism and Multiculturalism in US." *Christian Science Monitor* 84, no. 95 (April 10, 1992), 11.

"The Importance of Ancestry." *The Oprah Winfrey Show*. Television Broadcast. ABC, Chicago, March 9, 2010.

"Is the Magic Gone from Black Studies at Harvard?" *The Journal of Blacks in Higher Education*, Autumn 2004, 91.

Jaggi, Maya. "Henry the First." *The Guardian*, July 6, 2002, http://www.guardian.co.uk/books/2002/jul/06/internationaleducationnews.highereducation.

Kalb, Claudia, and Mark Starr. "Education: Up from Mediocrity—Now Black Studies at Harvard Is Famous for Its Stars." *Newsweek* 127, no. 8 (February 19, 1996), 64.

Leatherman, Courtney. "Perceived Slight May Produce a Gain for Yale's African-American Studies Program." *Chronicle of Higher Education* 46 (February 25, 2000), A18.

Lubiano, Wahneema. "Henry Louis Gates, Jr., and African-American Literary Discourse." *New England Quarterly* 62, no. 4 (December 1989), 561.

Magner, Denise K. "Nomadic Scholar of Black Studies Puts Harvard in the Spotlight." *Chronicle of Higher Education* 38, no. 45 (July 15, 1992), A13.

Malveaux, Julianne. "Bostonians Squabble over Headline." *Black Issues in Higher Education* 15, no. 7 (May 28, 1998), 28.

Marriott, Michel Marriott. "Planet Africa: Black History on Disk; Henry Louis Gates Jr. and Microsoft Produce A Long-Awaited, Much-Debated Encyclopedia." *New York Times* (January 21, 1999), http://www.nytimes.com/1999/01/21/technology/planet-africa-black-history-disk-henry-louis-gates-jr-microsoft-produce-long.html?pagewanted=all&src=pm.

May, Lee. "Turning a New Page in History." *Los Angeles Times* 109 (May 14, 1990), A1.

Meyer, Bill. "White Cop Who Arrested Black Scholar Henry Louis Gates Taught Class on Racial Profiling to Police." *Cleveland Plain Dealer* (July 23, 2009), http://www.cleveland.com/nation/index.ssf/2009/07/white_cop_who_arrested_black_s.html.

Newman, Richard. "Henry Louis Gates Jr." *Publishers Weekly* 241, no. 25 (June 20, 1994), 80.

Offman, Craig. "The Making of Henry Louis Gates, CEO." *Salon* (June 16, 1999), http://www.salon.com/books/it/1999/06/16/gates.

Ogletree, Charles. "Lawyer's Statement on the Arrest of Henry Louis Gates Jr." *The Root* (July 20, 2009), http://www.theroot.com/views/lawyers-statement-arrest-henry-louis-gates-jr.

"On U.S. Cultural Literacy: the Stakes and Strategy." *New York Times* 139 (December 6, 1989), B8(N), B14(L).

Parker, Laura. "Rap Lyrics Likened to Literature: Witness in 2 Live Crew Trial Cites Art, Parody, Precedents." *Washington Post* 113 (October 20, 1990), D1.

Rimer, Sara. "On Front Lines of Battle of Tradition and Change." *New York Times* 145 (March 20, 1996), A10(N), A14(L).

River, Eugene. "The Responsibility of Intellectuals in the Age of Crack." *Boston Review* (October 1992), http://www.bostonreview.net/BR17.5/rivers.php.

Shumway, David R. "The Star System in Literary Studies." *PMLA* 112, no. 1 (January 1997), 85.

Slaughter, Jane. "Henry Louis Gates Jr." *Progressive* 62, no. 1 (January 1998), 30.

Smith, Dinitia. "Centuries of Writing by Blacks Distilled Into a Single Volume." *The New York Times*, sec. C (December 12, 1996), 15.

Taylor, Ronald A. "Academic Theater: On the Road with Cornel West, Henry Gates and SRO Crowds." *Black Issues in Higher Education* 13, no. 5 (May 2, 1996), 12.

Taylor, Stuart. "Sotomayor, Gates and Race." *National Journal* (August 1, 2009), http://www.nationaljournal.com/njmagazine/or_20090801_5674.php.

Teachout, Terry. "Dead Center: The Myth of the Middle." *National Review* 44, no. 21 (November 2, 1992), 53.

Trescott, Jacqueline. "Harvard's Dream Team: Many of the Nation's Top Black Intellectuals Have Heeded the Call of Scholar Skip Gates. Now the Real Test Begins." *Washington Post* 119 (February 26, 1996), B1.

Ward, Jerry W., Jr. "Interview with Henry Louis Gates, Jr." *New Literary History* 22, no. 4 (Autumn 1991), 927.

White, Jack E. "The Black Brain Trust." *Time* 147, no. 9 (February 26, 1996), 58.

Wilson, Robin. "Family Revision." *The Chronicle of Higher Education* 52, no. 26 (March 3, 2006), http://go.galegroup.com/ps/i.do?id=GALE%7CA147062958&v=2.1&u=ches75568&it=r&p=EAIM&sw=w.

Yardley, Jonathan. "Back Where He Started From." *The Washington Post* (May 15, 1994), Book World, X3.

BOOKS BY HENRY LOUIS GATES, JR.

The African-American Century: How Black Americans Have Shaped Our Country. Co-written with Cornel West. New York: Free Press, 2000.

Afro-American Women Writers. New York: Macmillan Library Reference, 1998.

Black Literature and Literary Theory. Co-written with Catherine R. Stimpson. New York: Routledge, 1990.

Colored People: A Memoir. New York: Knopf, 1994.

Figures in Black: Words, Signs and the Racial Self. New York: Oxford University Press, 1987.

The Future of the Race. Co-written with Cornel West. New York: Knopf, 1996.

Loose Canons: Notes on the Culture Wars. New York: Oxford University Press, 1992.

The Signifyin(g) Monkey: Towards a Theory of Afro-American Literary Criticism. New York: Oxford University Press, 1988.

Speaking of Race: Hate, Speech, Civil Rights and Civil Liberties. New York: New York University Press, 1995.

Thirteen Ways of Looking at a Black Man. New York: Random House, 1997.

Truth or Consequences: Putting Limits on Limits. Worcester, MA: American Antiquarian Society, 1994.

Wonders of the African World. New York: Knopf, 1999.

WORKS EDITED BY HENRY LOUIS GATES, JR.

African American Studies: An Introduction to the Key Debates. Edited with Jennifer Burton. New York: W.W. Norton, 2002.

Africana: The Encyclopedia of the African and African American Experience. Edited with Anthony Appiah. Boulder, CO: Perseus Books, 1999.

Bearing Witness: Selections from African American Autobiography in the Twentieth Century. New York: Pantheon Books, 1991.

Black Imagination and the Middle Passage. Edited with Maria Diedrich and Carl Pederson. New York: Oxford University Press, 1999.

The Classic Slave Narratives. New York: New American Library, 1987.

The Dictionary of Global Culture. Edited with Anthony Appiah. New York: Knopf, 1995.

Identities. Edited with Anthony Appiah. Chicago: University of Chicago Press, 1996.

The Norton Anthology of African American Literature. Edited with Nellie Y. McKay. New York: W.W. Norton and Co., 1997.

The Oxford Companion to African American Literature. Edited with William L. Andrews, et al. New York: Oxford University Press, 1997.

Race, Writing, and Difference. Chicago: University of Chicago Press, 1986.

Reading Black, Reading Feminist: A Critical Anthology. Oklahoma City: Meridian Book, 1990.

Schomburg Library of Nineteenth-Century Black Women Writers. New York: Oxford University Press, 1991. (A 10-volume supplement).

ARTICLES AND OTHER CONTRIBUTIONS BY HENRY LOUIS GATES, JR.

"Academe Must Give Black Studies Programs Their Due." *Chronicle of Higher Education* 36, no. 3 (September 20, 1989), http://go.galegroup.com/ps/i.do?id=GALE%7CA7940861&v=2.1&u=ches75568&it=r&p=EAIM&sw=w.

"African American Studies in the 21st Century," *Black Scholar* 22, no. 3 (Summer 1992), 2.

"The African-American Century: A Reality That Is More Complicated and More Heroic Than the Myth." *The New Yorker* 72, no. 10 (April 29, 1996), 9.

"American Letters, African Voices: History of African American Authors." *New York Times Book Review* (December 1, 1996), http://astroweb.case.edu/heather/anthology.pdf.

"Beware of the New Pharaohs, Afrocentrism and Education," *Newsweek* 188, no. 13 (September 23, 1991), 47.

"Black Creativity: On the Cutting Edge." *Time* 144, no. 15 (October 10, 1994), http://www.time.com/time/magazine/article/0,9171,981564,00.html.

"The Black Leadership Myth," *New Yorker* 70, no. 34 (October 24, 1994), 7.

"Blacklash? African Americans Object to Gay Rights-Civil Rights Analogy." *The New Yorker* 69, no. 13 (May 17, 1993), 42.

"The Charmer, Louis Farrakhan," *New Yorker* 72, no. 10 (April 29, 1996), 116.

"Delusions of Grandeur: Young Blacks Must be Taught That Sports Are Not the Only Avenues of Opportunity." *Sports Illustrated* 75, no. 8 (August 19, 1991), 78.

"The Fire Last Time: What James Baldwin Can and Can't Teach America." *New Republic* 206, no. 22 (June 1, 1992), 38.

"Foreword" to *The Greatest Taboo: Homosexuality in Black Communities*. Edited by Delroy Constantine-Simms. Boston: Alyson Books, 2001.

"How Do We Solve Our Leadership Crisis?" *Essence* 35, no.9 (June 1996), 16.

"Introduction: Tell Me Sir, . . . What is 'Black Literature?' " *PMLA* 105, no. 1 (January 1990), 11.

"Just Whose 'Malcolm' Is It, Anyway?: Spike Lee's New Film Biography of Malcolm X." *New York Times* 141 (May 31, 1992), http://www.nytimes.com/1992/05/31/movies/film-just-whose-malcolm-is-it-anyway.html?pagewanted=all&src=pm.

"The Master's Pieces: On Canon Formation and the African-American Tradition." *South Atlantic Quarterly* 89, no. 1 (Winter 1990), 89–110.

"Muliculturalism and Its Discontents," *Black Scholar* 24, no. 1 (Winter 1994), 16.

"On Honoring Blackness," *American Enterprise*, 6, no. 5 (September–October 1995), 49.

"Our Next Race Question: The Uneasiness Between Blacks and Latinos." *Harper's*, 292, no. 175 (April 1, 1996), 55–63.

Personal History, "In the Kitchen," *The New Yorker* (April 18, 1994), 82.

"Thirteen Ways of Looking at a Black Man. African American Leaders React to the O. J. Simpson Trial and the Million Man March," *New Yorker* 71, no. 33 (October 1995), 56.

"2 Live Crew, Decoded: Rap Music Group's Use of Street Language in Context of Afro-American Cultural Heritage Analyzed." *New York Times* 139 (June 19, 1990), A23.

"What's in a Name: Some Meanings of Blackness," *Dissent* 36, no. 4 (Fall 1989), 487.

"Words that Wound: Critical Race Theory, Assaultive Speech and the First Amendment." *New Republic* 209, no. 12–13 (September 20, 1993), 37.

INDEX

About the Author

MEG GREENE is a historian and an award-winning writer. She holds an MA in history from the University of Nebraska at Omaha and an MS in historic preservation from the University of Vermont. She is the author of more than 30 books on a wide variety of history topics and biographies. *Henry Louis Gates, Jr.* is her fifth title for the Greenwood Biographies series. Ms. Greene makes her home in North Carolina.